The Language Hoax

The Language Hoax

Why the World Looks the Same in Any Language

John H. McWhorter

OXFORD
UNIVERSITY PRESS

OXFORD
UNIVERSITY PRESS

Oxford University Press is a department of the
University of Oxford. It furthers the University's objective
of excellence in research, scholarship, and education
by publishing worldwide.

Oxford   New York

Auckland   Cape Town   Dar es Salaam   Hong Kong   Karachi
Kuala Lumpur   Madrid   Melbourne   Mexico City   Nairobi
New Delhi   Shanghai   Taipei   Toronto

With offices in

Argentina   Austria   Brazil   Chile   Czech Republic   France   Greece
Guatemala   Hungary   Italy   Japan   Poland   Portugal   Singapore
South Korea   Switzerland   Thailand   Turkey   Ukraine   Vietnam

Oxford is a registered trade mark of Oxford University Press
in the UK and certain other countries.

Published in the United States of America by
Oxford University Press
198 Madison Avenue, New York, NY 10016

Library of Congress Cataloging-in-Publication Data
McWhorter, John H., author.
The language hoax : why the world looks the same in any language /
John H. McWhorter.
pages   cm
ISBN 978-0-19-936158-8 (hardcover : alk. paper)
1. Language and culture.   2. Sapir-Whorf hypothesis.   I. Title.
P35.M37 2014
306.44—dc23   2013033221

1 3 5 7 9 8 6 4 2
Printed in the United States of America
on acid-free paper

For Dahlia

CONTENTS

INTRODUCTION

THIS BOOK IS A manifesto. I will oppose an idea about language that took hold among certain academics starting in the 1930s, and of late has acquired an unseemly amount of influence over public discussion as well. This is the idea that people's languages channel the way they think and perceive the world.

You may be familiar with it. Among memories of your readings over the past ten years, for example, may dwell Amazonian tribespeople described as unable to do math because their language doesn't have numbers. Or you may have read about people who have the same word for *green* and *blue*, who we are to imagine not perceiving the difference in color between a leaf and the sky as vividly as we do. The whole idea is a kind of ongoing promo from the worlds of linguistics, anthropology, and psychology, the ad jargon typified by the subtitle of Guy Deutscher's *Through the Language Glass*, "Why the world looks different in other languages."

The notion is, for better or for worse, mesmerizing. Just think—what we speak is what we are. We are the language we speak.

This is true, of course, to an extent. A take-home insight from the idea that language channels thought is that a language's words and grammar are not just a random constellation, but are the software for a particular culture. No one could deny that there is some truth in that. In Thai, there are different words for *you* according to seven different grades of formality, and to not use them is not to be Thai, unless you are a child or new to the language. To pretend this has nothing to do with the highly stratified nature of Thai society in the past and present would be peculiar.

Vocabulary also reflects cultural concerns and not only in obvious areas such as technology and slang. Few people could be truly intrigued that we have names for computer components and salty terms relating to things like dating and social mores. However, quieter things say more than we always notice. Once, while staying at a hotel in the Bahamas I noticed a rather lovely cat gliding around outside. A Caribbean I was with said, "Oh, that must be the hotel cat." That is, a cat who lives more or less around the place and serves as an unofficial mascot. I had never heard of a hotel cat. It would never occur to me to put "hotel" and "cat" together, and in fact, to me part of the essence of the hotel experience would seem to be an absence of cats.

However, that my friend would mention a *hotel cat* suggested that the relationship between felines and hotels was different depending on where I was. Even a detail in the way he said it gave away that he was referring to something culturally entrenched: he didn't accent it as "hotel CAT," but as "ho-TEL cat." If you think about it, the second way of saying it means hotel cats are, as one says these days, "a thing." Think of how we say ICE cream rather than iced CREAM—as one did when it was a novelty, or CELL phone rather than cell PHONE—as I recall people saying in the early 1990s. In two-word expressions, the accent tends to shift backward when something becomes "a thing"—that is, culture! From the Caribbean man's one utterance—and not even a foreign one—I learned that mascot cats at hotels were a component of the local culture.

But the "language as thought" idea refers to much more than what qualifies it to its speakers as "a thing." We are to suppose that the way a language's grammar works, and the way it applies words to even mundane objects and concepts, shapes how its speakers experience life in ways far beyond desserts and gadgets. Hotel cats—sure, but what about a language that gives you a whole different sense of time than anything we can spontaneously imagine, even if we are from the Bahamas?

* * *

This all became a going concern with Benjamin Lee Whorf's proposition in the 1930s that the Native American language Hopi has no way to mark time—no tense markers, no words like *later*—and that this corresponded with the Hopis' sense of how time and the world work. English obsesses with placing events in the present, past, or future, Whorf argued, in contrast to a language like Hopi with no present, past, and future. In Whorf's sense of Hopi, present, past, and future are in essence the same, corresponding to the cyclical sense of time in Hopi cosmology. Thus it's not by chance that Hopi has no equivalent to English's between *walk, walked,* and *will walk*: it's about thought patterns. Culture. In Hopi, whether it's about yesterday, to-morrow, or right now, you just walk.

Whorf was a fire inspector by day, and perhaps coming to linguistic study from the outside made him more likely to come up with out-of-the-box insights than would a card-carrying linguist. Because of Whorf's pioneering role in the field of linguistics, the whole idea has been coined *Whorfianism*, or the *Sapir-Whorf hypothesis*—Edward Sapir was a mentor of Whorf's who found the idea similarly compelling—or, among academics, *linguistic relativity* and *linguistic determinism*.

Under any name, the idea that grammar channels people into thinking of time as cyclical is catnip. Even a well-fed hotel cat would eat it up. Or a college student, such as the one I once was. I got a dose of this version of Hopi linguistic anthropology in 1984, and it is now the sole thing I remember from the class, except that we read some of *The Last of the Mohicans* and that the teacher—a Tom Petty lookalike—seemed ineffably sad.

Whorf, however, wasn't, and he had an agenda, laudable in itself. He wanted to show that people dismissed even by the educated as "savages" in his time were as mentally developed as Westerners are. His was an era when, for example, none other than the *Webster's Second New International Dictionary*, cherished as a staple of the proper middle-class home, defined Apaches as "of warlike disposition and relatively low culture."

Yet, as with so many tantalizing and even well-intentioned notions, this conception of the Hopi language turned out to be wrong. Hopi marks time as much as anyone would expect a language to, with good old-fashioned tense markers and plenty of words for things like *already* and *afterward*. Furthermore, attempts over the next few decades to reveal Native Americans as cognitively distinct from Westerners because of mental filters exerted by their languages never bore fruit.

For example, if in Navajo, there are different words for *move* depending on whether it is one, two, or several people doing the moving, does that mean that Navajos have a thing about moving as central to existence? Linguist Harry Hoijer thought so in the 1960s. His overall career was invaluable in documenting fascinatingly complex languages on the brink of extinction, but he, a disciple of Edward Sapir as Whorf had been, was open to Whorfianism to an extent not uncommon among Native American language specialists of his time. When it came to Navajo, he linked its proliferation of *move* verbs to Navajos' nomadism in the past, and even to figures in their mythology "moving" to repair the dynamic flux of the universe.

But wait: what about all of the other languages in the world that also happen to get particular about going and moving? In Russian how you say *go* is so complicated that whole books are written about it and it's one of the last things nonnative learners manage to get right. The word is different depending on whether you walked or rode, and then after you have that figured out, it is different depending on whether you came back after you went, in addition, all of the forms are irregular. Yet nomadism is not exactly central to the Russian soul, and the last time I checked, Russians' interest in repairing the dynamic flux of the universe seemed rather low.

Yet beyond obscure academic journals it's easy to miss how poorly the Whorfian idea has fared scientifically. Of late especially, popular books such as Daniel Everett's *Don't Sleep, There Are Snakes*, Deutscher's *Through the Language Glass*, well-publicized studies by Stanford psychologist Lera Boroditsky, and other works have established a Whorfian meme in public discussion. It is easy to suppose that one of the most interesting things about language is that people whose languages assign genders to inanimate objects perceive those objects as meaningfully more male or female than speakers of English (how things marked neuter fit into this I have never quite understood), or that Russians are more meaningfully sensitive to the difference between dark blue, light blue, and green than Koreans, who have a single word that covers both blue and green.

* * *

Crucially, a connection between language and thought does exist. The problem is how that connection has percolated into public discussion, reminiscent of how the rumor mill magnifies the blip into a cataclysm. For example, the ideas about gender and colors, plus some other intersections between language and thought, have been studied by a new generation of researchers with a much more measured approach than Whorf's. Their experiments are clever and elegant, and only the most rabid skeptic could deny that their work has shown a connection between language and thought. Yet most would consider it a fair assessment that the work of this cohort, often termed the "Neo-Whorfians," has shown that language's effect on thought is distinctly subtle and, overall, minor. Not uninteresting—but nevertheless, minor. This, however, is not the easiest conclusion to get excited about outside of academia, and unsurprisingly, the public gets a rather spicier take on the issue.

To be sure, both Deutscher's and Everett's books actually argue that language's effect on thought is modest, hedging the issue as responsibly as we would expect of academics. Both are well aware that the classic formulation of Whorfianism is hopeless. Everett's point is, in fact, more that culture can shape language—essentially an extension of the *hotel cat* phenomenon—than the other way around. By the end of his book, Deutscher even spells out that "Color *may* be the area that *comes closest* in reality to the metaphor of language as a lens,"—italics mine—making clear that overall, evidence for "language as a lens" has been elusive. *Through the Language Glass* is so thorough in outlining both the failure of early Whorfianism and the deeply modest results of Neo-Whorfianism that it is, in essence, a gorgeously written chronicle of an idea that didn't pan out. Truly gorgeous: the prose is the written equivalent to foie gras or, if that's not up your alley, key lime pie.

However, the problem is that the media, as well as the public, *want* the idea to have panned out. The language-as-thought idea vibrates in tune with impulses deeply felt in the modern enlightened American's soul. Ethnocentrism revolts us. Virtually as penance for our good fortune in living in a wealthy and geopolitically dominant society, as well as for the horrors we have perpetrated on so many groups in the world, we owe it to the rest of the world to stress our awareness that the less fortunate are our equals. We Westerners are "so white"—a cultural self-condemnation that would baffle a Western time traveler from as recently as 1960. We look with a certain envy at the vibrant diversity, and even authenticity, of the rest of the world.

Attractive, then, will be the idea that each language is its own mind-altering cocktail. All of us are seeing, as it were, different colors ("Man, the colors! The colors!"). Just imagine all of the untapped ideas and perspectives out there among peoples we generally hear too little about, as well as among ones we see every day. We Westerners have learned our lesson: we are only one way of being human, and not the best one, much less the most important in the grand scheme of things. Under Whorfianism, everybody is interesting and everybody matters.

Under this impulse, the general impression from the media coverage of the relevant books, their blurbs, and what readers are therefore led to seek in them (or assume is in them) is that language does channel thought in a dramatic way, and that this is a fascinating new discovery from experts on language and related subjects. Deutscher's and Everett's books, for example, are primarily known as books that show that language shapes thought, not as gingerly explorations with tentative conclusions. That misimpression is easy to fall into. A valedictory passage such as Everett's that "We all possess grammars of happiness—our identities and our cultural cloaks," warmly memorable, exemplifies the aforementioned catnip. The cozy "cloak" analogy suggests—and imprints—a snugger bond between language and thought than Everett actually subscribes to.

Or, more were exposed to Deutscher through a widely read op-ed summary of his book than through the book itself, and in that piece we learned that humans "acquire certain habits of thought that shape our experience in significant and often surprising ways." But there is a short step between this and Whorf's idea that while Western language led to the insights of Isaac Newton, Hopi grammar suggests the next step in science, "a NEW LANGUAGE by which to adjust itself to a wider universe"—and the layman could easily fail to even perceive the step at all.

There are questioning voices, to be sure. For example, Steven Pinker artfully deconstructs the dramatic readings from the Neo-Whorfian studies in a section of his magisterial *The Stuff of Thought*. However, as this is but one of myriad insights in Pinker's cornucopia of a volume, the books and articles focused solely on "language as a lens" make the louder noise.

Not that the louder noise is even a crude one. Even Whorfianism's biggest fans regularly disown the old-time "Hopi" version. It is typical—seemingly almost required—to quote founding linguist Roman Jakobson, whose verdict was that "languages differ essentially in what they *must* convey and not in what they *may* convey." The insight is that languages do not saddle speakers with blinders preventing them from perceiving what their vocabularies and grammars happen not to call attention to. Yes, one language forces one to speak gender, such as English with *he* and *she*; many languages have one word that covers both men and women. Yes, another one forces one to speak social hierarchy, such as Thai and all of those ways of saying *you*, or even European languages like French with the difference between familiar *tu* and formal *vous*. Yet, one *can* say anything in any language. Even people new to the topic often come up with this basic insight on their own.

However, within the cultural context of our times, so hungry for confirmation that grammar is a pair of glasses, the Jakobson quote lends itself readily to a less temperate interpretation than Jakobson intended. Sure, anyone *can* say anything—but couldn't those things that a language *must* convey constitute a "worldview," fascinatingly distinct from our own? We can know that all people *can* think the same things, while also hoping that there is some magical degree to which they in fact do not. "Surely the question is worth asking..." one might hear—and it has been asked, for almost eighty years now. The verdict has long been in, and yet the impression persists that there remains a question to be asked—*in perpetuo*, it would seem.

Nominally we are fascinated by a question as to *whether* language influences thought in a significant way. However, in the way the question is framed and reported on, there reigns a tacit assumption that the answer to this question cannot be no.

* * *

However, the whole notion that how someone's language works determines, in any significant way, how they see the world is utterly incoherent, and even dangerous. Therefore, I have two goals in this book.

One will be to complement the opposing case from psychology, such as Steven Pinker's, with one from linguistics, showing why this idea of languages as pairs of glasses does not hold water in the way that we may, understandably, wish it did. This becomes clear from a perspective encompassing the world's languages rather than just a few at a time, upon which we see how Whorfianism forces us into endless contradictions, unwitting disparagement of billions of the world's human beings, and even cartoonish perspectives about ourselves. We will see that a broader perspective on languages makes one glad that the Neo-Whorfian studies don't support the "language as a lens" theory any more than they do—glad to an extent that if they were more supportive, you would likely consider the public better kept in the dark about it.

Then second, not only does a full representation of how languages work show how utterly unworkable the idea is that Language X makes its speakers see and feel "a different world" than speakers of Language Y, but in the end, the embrace of this idea is founded on a quest to acknowledge the intelligence of "the other," which, though well intentioned, drifts into a kind of patronization that the magnificent complexity and nuance of any language makes unnecessary. It is a miracle when any one of the world's six billion persons utters a sentence, quite regardless of whether it signals how they "see the world."

Our impulse to identify and celebrate what we call *diversity* begins as noble, but it is too little acknowledged how dangerous this quest becomes. Besides the alarmingly fine line between diversity and diorama, more than a few whom few of us could break bread with today have found the "language as a lens" idea attractive. Take the intransigent ultranationalist German historian Heinrich von Treitschke. Prussophile, xenophobic, and nakedly anti-Semitic, he was given in the late nineteenth century to insights such as "differences of language inevitably imply differing outlooks on the world." You can imagine the kinds of arguments and issues he couched that kind of statement in, and yet the statement itself could come straight out of Whorf, and would be celebrated as brain food by a great many today. "Surely," after all, "the question is worth asking..."—yet somehow, we would rather von Treitschke hadn't, and find ourselves yearning for thoughts about what we all have in common.

In that vein, my message is not a negative one in the end.

The other goal of this book will be to show that we can vibrantly acknowledge the intelligence and sophistication of indigenous peoples in another way: by stressing that all humans are mentally alike. Languages viewed in a worldwide sense show this much more clearly than they reveal six thousand distinct "worldviews" and point us to the larger and ultimately more useful truth. Language is a lens indeed—but upon humanity much more than upon humanities. Here's why.

The Language Hoax

CHAPTER 1

Studies Have Shown

My goal in this manifesto is straightforward. I wish to show the flaws in, and even dangers of, the more sensational implications bandied about in our intellectual culture over whether and how language shapes thought. However, in this first chapter I need to ward off a possible misinterpretation, to the extent that this is possible.

I may be taken as dismissing the work of Neo-Whorfians, but I mean no such thing. I seek out the articles in question and read them with great joy. As far as I can assess, they are composed with great care, enviable imagination, and thorough training. In my teaching, I regularly note that new Whorfian work has shown some modest effects that one might want to know about.

What I take issue with is the tendency to interpret this work as suggesting something about the human condition that I think it does not. To be sure, this interpretation is one more talked about after the fact—by some of the authors and certainly by onlookers—than is actually engaged within the experiments themselves. Yet this interpretation, ripe for cocktail party chat, media-friendly, and beckoningly interdisciplinary, has much greater impact than the minutiae of the experiments. It requires, then, engagement and critique—even with full respect for the work itself.

Ultimately, almost all books settle into the public consciousness in shorthand. I assume that this book, if cited, will often be classed as simply dismissing Neo-Whorfianism. Regardless, I would be remiss without making my actual position clear for those engaging the text.

Hitting a Wall after a Long Night

One of my favorite Neo-Whorfian experiments is one the public doesn't hear much about, perhaps because it doesn't involve concepts quite as immediately enticing as colors and genders. Yet this experiment is flawlessly constructed, easy to understand, and exemplifies perfectly what good Neo-Whorfianism is—and isn't—about.

It hinges on a difference between languages that one would be unlikely to consider important in the daily scheme of things. In English we say a *long time*. In Spanish, one says *mucho tiempo*, a lot of time. If you put it as "a long time," *un tiempo largo*, no one will throw you off a bus, but it's ungainly, not true español. In English, time is a distance. In Spanish, it's an amount or a size.

Greek is the same way: you don't have a long night in Athens, you have a big one, a "lot of" night. We might be tempted to read the Greek expression metaphorically—we have "big" nights in English, too, but Greeks don't mean that the way we do. For example, in Greek you also have a "big" relationship rather than a long one, and what they mean by that is that the relationship lasted a long time. As in Spanish, time is stuff, something there can be a lot of, rather than a stretching out of something. "Long" night in Greek is weird Greek.

But then, in Indonesian it's as in English: long times, long nights. These things vary from language to language: French is like English and Indonesian, while Italian is like Spanish and Greek.

One might suppose that a difference like this would be a mere matter of "feel" for the language in question and of no import beyond that. It's what I would once have assumed. However, show an English speaker—who says a "long" time—a line slowly lengthening toward an end point on a screen, and then a square slowly filling up from bottom to top, and she's better at guessing how long it will take the line to hit the end than for the square to be full. Yet a Spanish speaker is better with the square filling up than the line reaching its end! Plus, with their "a lot of night," Greeks pattern with Spanish speakers and Indonesians with their "long" nights pattern like English speakers.

Among the reasons one might come up with for this difference, clearly the most plausible one is language: the metaphor for time in people's language determined their performance on the test. Try fashioning an idea that Spanish, Greek, and Italian pattern together because of something about Mediterranean culture, and notice how hard it is to come up with how the beauties of the water and the splendiferousness of the seafood would make people better at predicting how long it will take before something is full. Then, good luck figuring out what cultural trait they have in common that would lessen people's knack at the same task among people in Paris, Leeds, and Jakarta!

This guessing experiment was constructed by Daniel Casasanto, a psychology professor at the University of Chicago. He persuasively argues that a case like this, in which people are not asked about language during the experiment and thus were not primed to use their language's expressions to help them make decisions, shows that language can shape thought. However, he makes no claims beyond this. After all, imagine what the claim would be. Speaking Greek creates a distinct mental world in which, well, you're a little better at predicting how quickly a space will fill up with liquid, while speaking Indonesian makes you a little better at the always handy skill of predicting just when something's going to hit a wall? How do those skills extend to life as it is lived—that is, to What It Means to Be Human? The Spanish speaker with his *mucho tiempo* walks about on a Saturday afternoon seeing his environment differently from me with my *long time* in that he . . . what?

Yet while writing *The Stuff of Thought*, Steven Pinker had to stop telling people he was writing a book about language and thought because regularly people assumed it must be about language as a lens—that is, about the structure of your language making you see the world "diversely" from other people. The cachet of this notion is not founded on findings of the kind Casasanto so elegantly identified, but on a tacit notion that such things are just preludes to something grander. We are to assume that, to adapt Al Jolson's old catchphrase, we ain't seen nothin' yet, and that the payoff will be a confirmation that languages lend us worlds of different colors.

Kind of Blue

Yet the top-class Neo-Whorfian work on color, marvelous as it is in many ways, does not lend itself any more gracefully to the juicier, humanist angle of interpretation. For example, I forget why I know that the Russian word for "gay" is *goluboj*, but as it happens the word's basic meaning is "light blue." Not just blue, because there is another Russian word for the darker, navy, Prussian version of blue, *siniy*. There is no word that means just blue: in Russian, the sky and a blueberry are different colors.

A neat Neo-Whorfian experiment presented Russian speakers with various tableaus of three squares on a computer screen: one on top, the other two right below it. The squares were various shades of what English speakers call blue, occurring in twenty gradations stretching from dark to light blue. In each tableau, one of the bottom squares was the same shade as the top square, while the other bottom one was a different shade. The Russians were given a task: to hit a button when they identified which bottom square was the same shade as the top one.

It must have been pretty dull to take this little test, but the researchers were trying to get at something: whether having different terms for dark blue and light blue has any effect on perception—that is, can language shape thought? And they found that it did. For example, if the top square was dark blue and the stray, different-colored bottom square was a shade or three into the light-blue range, then the Russians hit the button in a flash, while if the stray square was just a different shade of dark blue the average time before hitting the button was longer. Things were the same the other way around: if the matching squares were light blue, then Russians hit the button without hesitation if the stray one was in the dark realm, but lingered otherwise.

Yet English speakers had the same response time wherever the stray square happened to fall in the blueness spectrum: a stray square's lightness didn't quicken them up when the matching squares were dark, and a stray square's darkness didn't quicken them up when the matching squares were light. This shows, in a really ingenious way, that having different terms for light blue and dark blue makes people differentiate those colors more quickly than people whose language has a single term for blue—and even when no one asks them about the words in question or even uses them.

Just in case anyone tried to find, say, some cultural reason why Russians would be more sensitive to the difference between dark blue and light blue than Americans, the researchers did another version of the experiment, to show that language really is what drives the Russians' difference. The second experiment had the subjects not only distinguish the stray square, but at the same time recite a random string of numbers they had just been asked to memorize. The mental candlepower required of doing that puts a temporary block on the processing of language, and in this version of the experiment, suddenly whether the stray square was of the other kind of blue made no difference in the response times. So, without language, Russians were no more attuned to the difference between dark blue and light blue than a guy from Atlanta.

But. A current fashion advertises this kind of test as showing that what your language is like makes you see the world in a particular way. The Anglophone, intrigued, will strain gamely to imagine what the world must look like through the eyes of someone to whom light blue and dark blue are "more different" than they are to them. The attempt may be reminiscent of trying to picture a fourth dimension.

But there's a problem. It's not that this experiment by Jonathan Winawer, Nathan Witthoft, Michael Frank, Lisa Wu, Alex Wade, and Lera Boroditsky isn't extremely clever, nor is it that it doesn't show that language affects thought. Rather, we hit a snag when we try to go beyond the experiment and embrace the notion that it is telling us something about worldviews, being human, and the like. Namely, when I described the difference in reaction times, I used vague terms such as *in a flash* and *linger*. However, in actuality, to seriously evaluate what this experiment means beyond the world of academic psychology, it must be clear what the mean difference in reaction time was, depending on which color direction the stray square leaned toward. It was—wait for it—124 milliseconds.

124 milliseconds! When the matching squares were darker, if the stray square was also in the dark realm, then Russians hit the button just *one tenth of a second* more quickly than if the stray square was in the light realm. They didn't linger for half

a minute, or even a whole second, or even a half second. Really, we can't even call a tenth of a second a linger at all.

Now, that there was an effect at all is still something—in itself. Think: among English speakers, just because of a difference in the language, there was no lag at all. But: upon what grounds are we to take a 124-millisecond difference in reaction time as signaling something about the way Russians *experience life*? Language affects thought? Apparently so, but as with so much in life, the issue is degree. At the current state of our knowledge, it would seem that *goluboj* is relevant to a Russian's soul more vividly in terms of sexual preference than color!

Intuition corresponds with the 124-millisecond figure in suggesting that we are not dealing with anything like different glasses. Upon learning that Russian has separate terms for dark and light blue, it would seem that some are inclined to wonder whether it means that Russians see a robin's egg and a preppy blazer as more distinct in color than English speakers do. However, to just as many English speakers, or, I highly suspect, more, the reaction is a certain bemusement that a language would make such a distinction. "Why would a language *need* to do that?" we might ask. "We certainly know that the color behind the stars on the American flag is starkly different from baby blue—but we don't need different words for it!" That's certainly how I felt when I first encountered Russian.

In that light, there are plenty of languages that do not make color distinctions an English speaker considers fundamental, in which case, to them, English looks as needlessly obsessive as Russian does to us. The Herero people of Namibia in Africa speak a language in which one term refers to both green and blue. Finding out that other languages have separate words for green and blue, the Herero were not given to wondering whether Westerners saw a different world than they. Rather, they were quite aware of the difference between the color of a leaf and the color of the sky—living on the land as they do would seem to have made it rather difficult to avoid noticing it at least now and then. They just found the idea of a language having separate words for those colors, when they learned such languages existed, faintly silly.

Some might still be open to an idea that, on some level, there is a scale of sensitivity to color upon which Russians are high up, English speakers are middling, and the Herero are down on the bottom. That ranking will feel distasteful to most of us—and we will see how often Whorfianism's implications end up confronting us with similarly icky propositions when it's not us that the studies depict as fascinatingly dim. It seems hardly irrelevant that the Herero, in terms of clothing and decoration, give all indication of reveling in color—including distinct greens and blues—just as much as Westerners. Despite all this, it may well be that an experiment could show that the Herero language wires the brain in some way that leaves its speakers a few milliseconds slower to distinguish a blue-green Crayola crayon from a green-blue one than the typical person on the street in Chicago or Stuttgart (German has *grün* and *blau*). But in this, we have departed from any meaningful discussion of differences in souls.

Yet souls are what we think of in response to statements like "As strange as it may sound, our experience of a Chagall painting actually depends to some extent on whether our language has a word for blue." That was one of the most resonant phrases in the editorial based on Deutscher's book and elicits almost 5,000 hits on Google at the moment I am writing this. As I have long experienced, the media (including publishers) tend to encourage academics to put things in that kind of way, in an endless quest for "eyes" (web hits). There are so many books out there; one must ballyhoo a bit. Editorials—and jacket copy—advertising the book will always have a certain rhapsodic quality that almost no actual text could embody.

However, phrases like the one about Chagall have more influence than the book itself, especially given the inherent frisson of the Whorfian idea, and it implies something the studies simply do not. Would lacking a word for blue really impact one's experience of a Chagall more than education, experience, or even mere variation between individuals' receptivity to art? The editorial did say only "to some extent," but let's face it, a hedge like that gets lost amid the sexy pull of the basic statement. The real question is to what "extent"? 124 milliseconds?

Tribe without Paper or Pencils Mysteriously Weak at Portraiture

There have been some claims about language affecting thought and culture, which, if valid, would indicate much more dramatic effects than infinitesimal differences in mental processing. However, what they demonstrate is cultural traits that language reflects, like Thai words for *you*, not linguistic traits magically shaping the culture.

You wouldn't have known it in the summer of 2004. That summer is defined in my memory by three things. One is the melody my cell phone played when a text came through, as that was the summer I started texting. The second is a beautiful house plant, of a kind fashionable at the time in New York City, that proliferated its light green leaves all over my study's windowsill and down to the floor. The third was endless media reports of the people who can't do math because their language has no numbers.

This sounded off to me, like a song played with an off chord, or ice cream that has been in the freezer next to leftover linguini and clams, such that into the initial glow of strawberry or chocolate drifts a stray hint of garlic. The coverage was sparked by Columbia University psychologist Peter Gordon's work on the language of a tiny Amazonian tribe called the Pirahã, and the result was that today an obscure language of the Brazilian rain forest has been discussed in various books written for the general public, and was especially publicized by Daniel Everett. It is always good to see a language so unlike Western ones getting so much attention. Nevertheless, it was still perplexing to see one publication after another exclaiming how counterintuitive it was that a group of people who don't have numbers, don't count things, and aren't good at it if you try to make them do it. "Tribe without names for numbers cannot count" (*Nature*, August 19, 2004). "Experts agree that the startling result provides the strongest support yet for the controversial hypothesis that the language available to humans defines our thoughts" (*New Scientist*, same day).

It's not that the Pirahã of the Amazon have been misportrayed. They really do not count and are all but hopeless at learning math. A Pirahã woman genuinely cannot tell you how many children she has, because the language has no words for numbers. There has been some controversy over just how utterly innumerate the Pirahã are. The evidence leaves me, for one, skeptical that they really have no concept of one and two, although it would appear that for them, "one" means what we would mean by "that there," and "two" is more a matter of "a pair and optionally one more or so." However, if someone lived with the Pirahã for several years as Everett did, then even if there is an extent to which people see what they want to see, we can take his word for it that the Pirahã don't talk about the numbers 5 or 42. If the Pirahã do by chance have counting games that they hid from Everett ("No, no, not in front of *him!*") then if all they have to work with is "that there" and "two and a bit" then we can assume that the game barely qualifies as what we think of as counting ("Here's one banana, Junior, and now, heeeeere's *something like two* bananas! Yaaay!!!!!").

The problem is the announcement, "Tribe without numbers in their language cannot do math," with breathless speculations about how the language shapes their existence. We have to imagine equivalent claims. "Tribe without letters cannot write": notice how unlikely such a headline seems. Not having letters would seem to be the very essence of not writing. When we encounter a group without writing, we speculate as to the historical or cultural reasons that explain why they have not adopted it. What would we think of someone who was instead mesmerized with the fact that the group have no conception of letters, seeing it as a valuable insight that this ignorance of letters is what prevents the people from writing anything down or being much good at trying to do so if asked? "Illiteracy prevents writing," the headlines announce—and we wonder whether we have had a small stroke.

Certainly not having numbers in your language will make learning math difficult. However, the fact that the language lacks numbers is not an independent variable in the way that having different words for dark blue and light blue or saying *big night* instead of *long night* are. Pirahã lacks numbers for a reason: an isolated hunter-gatherer culture has no need for a word for 116, or to do long division, or to speculate about the nature of zero.

If, nevertheless, Pirahã were the only language in the world to lack numbers, then there would be a case for treating it as a fluky matter with fluky consequences. That is, we might suppose that there are tribes who have no number words but still count to 7 or 54 silently with their fingers or by lining up little buds on the ground. However, as we would expect, small hunter-gatherer groups quite often have no numbers beyond two or so. That doesn't get around much; only because the groups are small ones unknown beyond where they reside. Many of them, in fact, live in the Amazon. Hence it's not that there is a mysterious lack of numbers in the language of one group that makes them bad at math. Rather, the lesson is that counting, as humanity goes, is an accessory, despite how fundamental it seems to us. Indigenous hunter-gatherers don't need to count, and thus often their languages have no word for the number 307.

An interesting thing to know, but building a case for language "shaping thought" is out the window. "Tribe without cars doesn't drive" sounds like something out of *Monty Python*, as does, really, the idea of marveling that people without numbers don't take to math. For example, cultures differ in the degree to which they happen to elaborate their music, art, or food. All people have and cherish these things to an extent, but, for example, some groups take cuisine to a more prolific and universally captivating level than others. Take Italy versus Romania, perhaps. Yes, I know Romanian food has its moments. New York diner menus even feature something I've never quite got around to eating called "Roumanian Steak." But still.

Suppose we encountered a tribe whose approach to food was relatively utilitarian, and found that in their language there was a single word that covered meat, vegetables, starches, and fruit. The person who came away saying that the reason these people weren't gourmands was that they didn't have words for different kinds of food would likely be a clever child, whom we would correct while chuckling warmly. Obviously, the cultural trait created the linguistic one.

Upon which we return to the likes of "Tribe's not playing music is traced to their lack of musical instruments." It is the warm attraction so many have to the idea of language shaping thought that leads people to treat this kind of reasoning as normal when it comes to language. Steven Pinker gets it just right: "The idea that Eskimos pay more attention to varieties of snow *because they have more words for it* is so topsy-turvy (can you think of *any other reason* why Eskimos might pay attention to snow?) that it's hard to believe it would be taken seriously were it not for the feeling of cleverness it affords at having transcended common sense."

It Depends on Where You Stand

It's hard to avoid the same verdict on a case that was often advertised as *the* one for skeptics to beat when the Neo-Whorfian work started getting attention beyond academic psychologists in the late 1990s. As always, the literature starts with something you wouldn't want to go through life not knowing, but then veers off into garlic ice cream.

There are groups in Australia who don't think of things being in front of, behind, to the left of, or to the right of them. Rather, they think of north, south, west, and east. Always. Not just when they turn north, and not just when a reason comes up to explicitly figure out which way is up. To a group like the Guugu Yimithirr (the name, in their language, roughly meaning "talking like this"), if a tree is in front of them and to the north, then they say it's north of them, and even when they turn around, they do not say it's behind them—they say it's north, which it still is. In front of them is now south, and they would describe a wall they might now be facing as "south." This is how they describe where things are inside, outside, in the dark, in a room they've never been in: they can always instantly discern wherever they end up as north, south, west, or east.

It makes perfect sense; it's just not what we would do. Here is a fascinating example of human diversity indeed. However, the scholars who have publicized this aspect of the Guugu Yimithirr call it stunning evidence for Whorfianism. Namely, they think of this not as something interesting about the Guugu Yimithirr as people but as something interesting about their language. To them it's not that the Guugu Yimithirr process direction differently than others do—it's that their language forces them to.

That is, "Tribe with no words for clothing do not wear clothes." Imagine: according to *Scientific American*, "Previously elusive evidence that language shapes thought has been discovered in Papua New Guinea, where the Stnapon tribe, who habitually wear no clothes, have been found to exhibit this trait because their language has no words for clothing." Unlikely— we assume that not wearing clothes came first, and that unremarkably the language developed no words for clothing.

In the same way, a Guugu Yimithirr man processes direction the way he does because his environment forces him to. The language part is just a result. Of course this is hardly a language that would *encourage* someone to think about *behind* and *beside*. But just as Eskimos have a reason to focus on snow, the Guugu Yimithirr have a reason to rely heavily on geographical coordinates: they live on flat land in the bush. In fact, this kind of reckoning is common in Australian Aboriginal languages.

I am hardly the first person to see it that way, but defenders insist that the language must be the driving force because there are similar cultures that do not rely on geographical coordinates. They posit that this means that it can't be culture that creates this orientation, therefore leaving language as where it all starts. This reasoning, however, would not stand up in court.

No one has ever claimed that a given cultural trait *always* expresses itself in a group's language. If it did, then every language spoken by a group with a strong sense of social hierarchy would have seven ways of saying *you*—even feudal European languages. Yet not one European language is ever recorded as doing so.

All evidence shows that people like the Guugu Yimithirr process the world as they do because of their environment, not their language. It is not even, as some might wonder, a chicken and egg case in which both sides are right. Exhibit A: There is no language like Guugu Yimithirr spoken in, for example, a rain forest or a town. People only rely on geographical coordinates to this extent in environments that would naturally make it urgent. No peoples surrounded by structures and roads in front of and behind them mysteriously insist on looking beyond them and saying "north" and "south."

Exhibit B: It is documented that among generations of Guugu Yimithirr who grow up outside of the indigenous environment, the geographical orientation quickly falls apart— this seems to have happened with countless Aboriginal groups. Again, what drives this way of speaking is where its speakers are, not the language.

But can't language play a part? Possibly, but the evidence suggests that it doesn't in any significant way. For example, languages index aspects of environment in other ways. In the Mayan language Tzeltal in Mexico, one refers to "uphill," "downhill," "across," and to place names rather than "in front of," "behind," and so forth. The Whorfian impulse starts with "What a fascinating language that channels its speakers into thinking that way!" However, more intuitively, we are also interested to know that the Tzeltal live on the side of a mountain!

Now, while some might try to save the Whorfian analysis by finding a group of people who live on the side of a mountain somewhere and yet speak and think in terms of left and right—"the language determines the thought pattern!"—there is another group that pretty much closes the case in favor of the prosecution. Upon which: Exhibit C: Next door to the Tzeltal live the Tzotzil, in the same kind of mountainside environment. As you might guess from the similarity of the names (one must guiltily admit they sound like two groups created by Dr. Seuss!), Tzeltal and Tzotzil are essentially variations on the same language: one, two, three is *hun, cheb, oxeb* in Tzeltal and *jun, chib, oxib* in Tzotzil. Yet the Tzotzil differ from the Tzeltal in that they do *speak* in left-right/front-back terms *linguistically*—yet if you submit them to a psychological experiment, they *still* reveal themselves to *conceptually* process direction in terms of geographical coordinates like the Tzeltal and the Guugu Yimithirr.

If a Tzotzil is presented with three objects laid out in a row on a table and is then asked to turn around to a table in back of them and arrange the objects "the same way," they will place them in a way that we would consider backward, as if the order of the objects on the first table were mirrored. For them, when they move, the world doesn't change—just like with the Tzeltal in the same experiment. What the Tzeltal and the Tzotzil have in common here is culture, not what their language—practically the same one—makes them do.

The cool insight is about the world, not what one's language makes you see in it. Processing direction geographically is something about culture, which can occur whether it penetrates language or not. Calling it language shaping thought looks plausible from the Tzeltal, but falls apart when we pull the camera back and bring in the Tzotzil. Calling it language shaping thought looks plausible from the Guugu Yimithirr point of view, but falls apart when we pull the camera back and bring in a hypothetical issue of the *Onion* with the headline "Legless Tribe Incapable of Walking Because They Have No Word for *Walk*."

Mommy, the Park Is Covered with Squirrel! Can I Go Feed Some of It?

And so it goes. I am unaware of a Neo-Whorfian study in which neither of these things are true: (1) it's hard to say what it has to do with what it is to be human, or (2) the whole claim is like saying a tribe's lack of a word for *calf* is why they don't raise cattle. The studies themselves are always intriguing, but if they are showing anything like different lenses on life, then the difference between the lenses is like the one between the two lenses that your optometrist shows you during an exam for glasses or contacts when you have to have her alternate between them several times to decide whether you see better through one or the other, because really, the chart looks the same through both. "Better? Or better? Better? Or better?" she says. "Well, uh…," one ventures. **E**, T X P R E, G J N B C… "Better? Or better?"—but actually you would experience life the same way in a pair of glasses fitted with either of them.

My praise of these studies in themselves is not a backhanded compliment. For example, there is work on Japanese that gets less attention than it should because it came along before the media happened to pick up on Neo-Whorfianism. It perfectly illustrates how Neo-Whorfianism can be great work despite offering little or nothing to those of a mystical bent.

In Japanese, when you talk about a number of something, the number has to come with a little suffix. That suffix is different according to what kind of thing or material something is. Two is *ni*, dog is *inu*. However, two dogs is not *ni inu*, but *ni-**hiki** no inu*. *Hiki* is used when you are talking about small animals and using a number. But if you say "two beers," *ni biru* is incomplete, and *ni-**hiki** no biru* would make the beer into a small animal. One neither pats, feeds, nor swats at a beer. You say *ni-**hon** no biru*, because *hon* is used for long, thin things, like bottles.

In Japanese this translates into saying "two little critter-nesses of dog," "two skinninesses of bottle." *Dog* and *bottle* are treated as substances, just as in English we say *two ounces of water* but *three pounds of meat*, except that in Japanese you have to do this with all nouns when accompanied by a number. In English only some nouns are substances: *three pounds of meat*, but we say *I have two desks in my office*, not *I have two woodnesses of desk in my office*, and *There are a lot of acorns over there*, not *Behold, there are many seednesses of acorn!* But whenever there's a number, woodnesses and seednesses are the lay of the land in Japanese.

There are dozens of these suffixes in Japanese. They are about the hardest things in the language, after getting used to the different word order, for English speakers to master because knowing which suffix to use for which noun gets a little arbitrary. Are bottles really long and thin in the way that pencils are? And when you find out *hon* also has to be used with phone calls and movies you just have to suck it up.

In any case, the Whorfian seeks to see if this grammatical trait, where everything is marked as stuff instead of as an object, has any reflection beyond. In fact, it does. In what is definitely the best-*smelling* Whorfian experiment yet, Mutsumi Imai and Dedre Gentner laid out for their subjects triads of objects: say, a C-shaped mass of Nivea (have you ever smelled Nivea? Truly heaven, I've always thought), a C-shaped mass of Dippity-Do (a hair gel more popular in the old days, which smells pretty good too, although currently they push an unscented kind, anyone's preference of which reminds me of people who poo-poo mackerel and sardines as "tasting like fish" as if that's a minus), and scattered little dapples of Nivea. Or a porcelain lemon juicer, a wooden lemon juicer, and then some pieces of porcelain (that part was just plain nice to look at).

Yes, all of this did apply to Whorfianism. Asked which two things go together out of the three, Japanese children were more likely to group the mass of Nivea with the little clumps of it, while American kids were more likely to group the similarly shaped masses of Nivea and Dippity-Do. The Japanese kids thought of the porcelain lemon juicer as forming a pair with the pieces of porcelain, while American kids grouped the two juicers and left those crummy shards of porcelain to the side. Americans group by shape, Japanese by material.

This is all the more fun because if you are American, you almost surely feel the American choices as more natural, even if you can see the basic sense in the Japanese kids' choices. Nivea with Nivea, well, of course! But to an American, somehow the fact that the two masses of Nivea and Dippity-Do are shaped alike "pops" more.

And wouldn't you know, when they hear about experiments like these, people who speak languages whose numbers work the Japanese way tend to find grouping by material more intuitive. That is even scientifically confirmed in experiments with other languages that treat all things as substances. Near Tzeltal and Tzotzil in Mexico is their relative language Yucatec, and its speakers have number suffixes like Japanese. Eight out of 10 of them given a paper tape cassette box (it was in the 1980s) group it with a small piece of cardboard, while 12 out of 13 English speakers grouped it with a plastic box. Yucatec speakers went by material, English speakers by shape.

One cannot assess Whorfianism without awareness of studies like these. Yet we must return to the big picture. Clearly, the Japanese and Yucatec experiments show that language can shape thought. The question is what is meant by thought. Many seek to read experiments like these as shedding light on larger issues: real life, the human condition. But what could that really mean from data of this sort? A difference in thought must be of a certain magnitude before it qualifies realistically as a distinct "worldview."

Is there anything a Japanese person has ever done in the 1,800 years since chopsticks have been used in that country, anything that any of the 125,000,000 Japanese do with chopsticks now, or anything that any Japanese-to-be will ever do with or even think about chopsticks, that seems even remotely traceable to them thinking of chopsticks as a substance rather than as a thing? That is, what effect of any kind has this mental trait ever had on a Japanese person's behavior, outlook, health, argumentational skill, artistic sensitivity, sexuality, or anything at all? "Goodness, this room is fairly bedecked with *chopstick*!"

At what shall we aim our subsequent experiments to find out how these Whorfian ripplets affect people and life as we know them? One can't help noting how few such experiments seem to actually occur. And if somewhere, somehow, Japanese people suggest that they think of chopsticks as a substance like water or sex in some stupendously minimal, ambiguous way—of the kind even scholars would likely have trouble even agreeing on anyway—why, really, should it occupy our attention long-term?

Any Whorfian study that suggests any effect on "worldview" less evanescent than this still meets trouble. For example, in Mandarin Chinese next month is "the month below" and last month was "the month above." Does that mean Chinese people think of time as stretching vertically rather than horizontally? Now, there would be a worldview—and for a while a paper by Stanford University psychologist Lera Boroditsky (last encountered heading that study of blueness in Russian) taught us that Chinese people do sense time as up and down, and the study comes up often in conversations about Whorfianism's plausibility.

In Boroditsky's experiment, Mandarin speakers were faster to answer a question like "August comes earlier than October" when they had just been shown pictures of objects oriented vertically (a ball over another one, for instance) rather than horizontally (worms following each other, for instance). However, I often noticed that the Chinese people I asked about this often said they didn't sense time as going up and down, and as it happens, various researchers have not been able to replicate Boroditsky's findings. Most indicatively, in one study English speakers were about even in terms of how well they did with sentences like "August comes earlier than October" depending on whether they had just seen vertically arranged balls or horizontally creeping worms.

To give up on a hypothesis upon the first volleys of criticism would be unscientific, and thus as expected, Boroditsky has refined her experimentation. In the latest rendition, subjects are asked to hit early/late buttons arranged vertically as well as horizontally in response to pictures (such as of a young and an old Woody Allen). Mandarin speakers are quicker when the buttons are vertical, paralleling the time expressions in their language.

But, we get back to the question as to what quick-*er* is and what it means. Mandarin speakers are 170 milliseconds faster at nailing "up" as previous. That is certainly a result. But then, English speakers are almost *300* milliseconds quicker at nailing what their language marks as previous, "left" over "right." And, even Mandarin speakers get "left" as earlier about 230 milliseconds faster—which we would expect since left-right time orientation exists alongside the up-down one in Mandarin.

So: English speakers register their language's way faster than Mandarin speakers register their language's way—and who knows why?—but even Mandarin speakers register the English way faster than their main one!!

So we do not know that Mandarin speakers "experience time vertically," and it is even precarious to leave it that they even experience time "more vertically," in that they demonstrably do at all, because let's face it, mental habit encourages letting that qualified assessment drift into the easier "Mandarin speakers feel time as up and down," period. What the studies show is that Mandarin speakers sense time primarily as horizontal, with a background openness to a sense of it as vertical that you can tease out from very, very careful experimentation.

Is that layered, subordinated twinge a "worldview"? In deciding whether it is, we must ask: where are the Mandarin speakers who say, "Oh, that isn't going to be ready for years and years!" pointing animatedly to the ground?

Language Is about All of Us

Yet no one would deny that human cultures are quite diverse, nor would anyone deny that the diversity means that humans of different groups experience life differently. However, language structure is not what creates this difference in experience. Culture certainly percolates into language here and there. Why would it not, since people with cultures speak language? However, language *reflects* culture—in terms of terminology, naturally, and also things like honorific levels of pronouns and geographical ways of situating oneself. But pronouns and topographical terms are, themselves, terminology in their way. They come for free from what life is like for a language's speakers.

What language does not do is shape thought by itself, in terms of meaningless gender divisions of the kind that in German makes forks female, spoons male, and knives something in between (*die Gabel, der Löffel, das Messer*), or in terms of how people see the world's colors, or in terms of whether we think of a cat as a clump of cuteness in the same way as we see a glorious-smelling white glob as a clump of Nivea. All attempts to find otherwise splutter. Even if you can, as it were, trick someone into revealing some queer little bias in a very clever and studiously artificial experiment, that weensy bias has nothing to do with anything any psychologist, anthropologist, or political scientist could show us about how the people in question manage existence.

Make no mistake: languages, like cultures, differ massively, and far beyond the terminological features that drift into them from the cultures. I have written about how vastly languages differ, and we will see it in the next chapters. The degree of divergence is awesome indeed: languages with only a handful of verbs (many Australian languages), languages with no regular verbs (Navajo), languages where a word's meaning differs according to nine different tones you utter it on (Cantonese), languages with only ten sounds (Pirahã again), languages with whole sentences that you need only one word to utter (Eskimo), languages with dozens of click sounds (did you ever read about the "Kung" "bushmen" in an anthropology class? "Kung" is actually lazy Westerner for !Xũũ where the ! is a click), languages with no tense at all (Maybrat in New Guinea), languages with two hundred genders (Nasioi, again in New Guinea), languages where the only ending in the present tense is the third-person singular one (English).

But the wonder is how in all of their diversity, these languages convey the same basic humanity. The cultural aspects qualify as scattered decoration. That will sound naïve to many—until they consider what it is to learn a language, upon which it becomes clear how ancillary the cultural aspect of a language is. How much of the Spanish or Russian or Chinese you hacked your way through was "cultural"?

If you want to learn about how humans differ, study cultures. However, if you want insight as to what makes all humans worldwide the same, beyond genetics, there are few better places to start than how language works. We will see why in subsequent chapters.

In this light, we must revisit some deeply seductive questions in Guy Deutscher's editorial based on his book: Did the opposite genders of "bridge" in German and Spanish, for example, have an effect on the design of bridges in Spain and Germany? Do the emotional maps imposed by a gender system have higher-level behavioral consequences for our everyday life? Do they shape tastes, fashions, habits, and preferences in the societies concerned? At the current state of our knowledge about the brain, this is not something that can be easily measured in a psychology lab. But it would be surprising if they didn't.

But what if they don't?

CHAPTER 2

Having It Both Ways?

PART OF WHY IT can seem so counterintuitive that language does not significantly "shape thought" is that it is so natural to suppose that fundamentally, what languages are like parallels what their speakers are like.

We could reasonably assume that the mechanics and nuances of the Burmese language correspond to being Burmese in some way that they do not correspond to being Icelandic. We may question the idea that language by itself shapes thought significantly, especially after reading the previous chapter. Yet we might assume that, nevertheless, cultures' thought patterns must somehow correspond to the languages they are couched in. After all, as I have specified, it isn't that culture *never* affects how language works. One could start with the Pirahã's innumeracy, meaning they don't have numbers, and then think of the Guugu Yimithirr's geographical needs and how they process front and back, and go from that to assuming that overall, what people are like is how their languages work. Not just in marginal splotches, but overall. Why not, really? Language is a part of a culture, and to speak, to express yourself, is what it is to *be*. It would certainly seem that the way a language works must reflect, then, what its people are like. Linguists are amply familiar with being asked whether this idea is true by students and by audience members in talks for the general public, and it fairly drips from a growing literature that calls attention to the number of obscure languages going extinct.

In that state of mind, seeking to make sense of things, it will be natural to assume that some kind of parallelism between language and what its speakers are like is salvageable with adjustment. As such, the Whorfian debate lends itself to an eternally useful approach: "Couldn't it work both ways?"

Thus: maybe to say that language creates thought, and therefore what a people are like, is oversimplifying. Yet language and thought could exist in a *complementary* relationship. Maybe a people's thoughts, their culture, have an effect on how their language works, whereupon it would then hardly be implausible that the language then reinforces the thoughts and the culture connected with them. Thus we can account for why trying to see things going in one direction from language to thought doesn't work: the reality could be more holistic.

That argument is reasonable. It is, more specifically, appealing. It gratifies one to identify a system rather than a mere one-way cause and effect. Eternally warned not to be reductive, and steeped in an intellectual culture that stresses webs, feedback loops, and complementarities in fields like ecology, evolution, and quantum physics, we seek the approach that entails mutual reinforcement, or, in a near-irresistible anthropomorphizing sense, cooperation. There is quiet yet potent rhetorical power here. Picture the gesture that often accompanies such propositions, rotating the hands around one another, and note how the mere sight of someone doing that makes you want to nod.

Even after some acquaintance with languages and linguistics, it will seem compelling to many that languages evolve to support the cultures of those who speak them. Like animals, languages evolve over time: dinosaurs became birds, Latin became French. Like animals, languages have family relationships: as manatees and dugongs are branches on one tree of mammal, French and Spanish are puppies in a brood born of Latin. Animals can go extinct, as can languages.

If so, then just as animals evolve according to the needs of their environment, then don't languages evolve according to the particular, culture-internal needs of their speakers?

Actually, no. Not in any significant way.

Words versus Whorfianism

That seems counterintuitive. *Languages evolve according to the needs of their speakers*: what could seem more unassailable? And yet the more one knows about languages in the worldwide sense, the more hopeless the proposition becomes.

This is not always easy to accept. At a talk I once gave on Whorfianism, an earnest student asked me, "But why would people have something in their language if they didn't need it?," clearly finding the notion otherwise almost off-putting. It's a good question, in that it points up the key juncture of misunderstanding: the very idea that language is primarily a cultural tool rather than primarily a shambolically magnificent accretion of random habits.

Note that I wrote "primarily." I should be clear that my claim is not that language is utterly divorced from practicality, or even from certain particularities of its speakers. Of course all languages serve the basic needs of communication. However, I doubt many find that counterintuitive, and it isn't the focus of Whorfianism. Who is impressed that a language has words for things, including churning out new ones as new objects emerge within the culture? Benjamin Lee Whorf certainly wasn't—he was on to something much more specific.

English has a word for canines of a certain sort: *dog.* English has words for more specific things important in the cultures that speak it: *computer, upload, blog,* and even quirkier things like *inferiority complex* and *jump the shark.* In the same way, Guugu Yimithirr makes heavy use of the words *north, south, west,* and *east* because direction is highly important to its speakers. That kind of thing, terminology for realities, is no more special in a tiny language spoken in the rain forest than it is in Los Angeles. It is quite different from the more mysterious and dramatic hypothesis that less concrete aspects of a language can make the world look more colorful, or time feel more vertical. Whorf was clear about this, referring to a person's

> unperceived intricate systematizations of his own language—shown readily enough by a candid comparison and contrast with other languages, especially those of a different linguistic family. His thinking itself is in a language—in English, in Sanskrit, in Chinese. And every language is a vast pattern-system, different from others, in which are culturally ordained the forms and categories by which the personality

not only communicates, but analyzes nature, notices or neglects types
of relationship and phenomena, channels his reasoning, and builds
the house of his consciousness.

Whorf, then, was referring to something deeper, and more
interesting, than the fact that rain forest people have names
for things that matter to them. He was supposing that the
very essence of how that people's language works, its
constructions, overall grammatical patterns, what would be
challenging in trying to learn how to form sentences in it, is
profoundly consonant with what it is to be them, rather than
anyone else.

If stressing instead the more mundane fact that a rain forest
people have words for their tools, customs, and concerns has
any purpose, it is not bolstering Whorfianism but dissuading
dismissive views of indigenous, unwritten languages. Make no
mistake, that problem is real: a traveler to Rossel Island off of
Papua New Guinea once had this to say about the "dialects"
she heard there: "Any that we heard were scarcely like human
speech in sound, and were evidently very poor and restricted
in expression. Noises like sneezes, snarls, and the preliminary
stages of choking—impossible to reproduce on paper—represented the names of villages, people, and things."

Yet the "dialects" she thought of herself as hearing were
one magnificent language, called Yélî Dnye, which is expressed
not in sneezes but in ninety different sounds, compared to
English's paltry forty-four. It has over one thousand prefixes
and suffixes, and it's hard to recognize "restricted" expression
in a language with, for example, eleven different ways of saying
"on" depending on whether something is on a horizontal

surface, a vertical one, a peak, whether something is scattered, whether something is attached to the surface, and so on.

However, I take the liberty of presuming that anyone reading this book readily sees the error in absurd caricatures such as the one of Yélî Dnye. An impression does persist even among the educated that unwritten, small languages are likely less complex than "real" languages like English and French (an impression I work against in *What Language Is*). However, no one interested in language thinks anyone goes about with a language little better than what animals are stuck with. As such, our interest in whether language evolves for the purposes of its speakers will concern the meatier Whorfian orientation. The question is not "Do languages develop words for things their speakers often talk about?" Of course they do, and we can move on to the more suspenseful question that really interests us: "Do languages evolve according to ways of thinking?"

Here is where a "complementary" take on Whorfianism might seem useful, especially since we know that external conditions *can* influence language—such as the Guugu Yimithirr direction words—and that conversely, language *can* influence how people process those external conditions, such as material markers in Japanese and Yucatec.

We might propose that just as Guugu Yimithirr has its directional marking because of its speakers' environment, the material suffixes in Yucatec must be there *because of* something in their environment that got them thinking that way in the first place. Then, if that works, certainly it is worth investigating whether among the Guugu Yimithirr the language also "reinforces" their sense of direction just as the sense of direction shapes their language. Thus we could see a kind of feedback loop—the culture affects the language, the language affects the culture, in a reciprocal relationship in which there is no point designating a chicken and an egg, at least not in the here and now.

The appeal of this "holistic" sense of language and thought would be in acknowledging that language does not create a "worldview" by itself while still preserving a sense that languages are like their speakers, and thus symptoms of diversity in the same way that cultures are. However, there is a fragility in the venture that tips us off to the reality. What would it be about the Yucatec's environment that led them to be more sensitive to what things are made of than Estonians, Mongolians, or especially, countless other Native American groups whose languages are not sensitive to material in the Yucatec way?

That is, if told that any of these other peoples actually were, as they in fact are not, more sensitive to what things are made of than English speakers, would we find it any more or less plausible than hearing of it about the Yucatec? And meanwhile, what could it be about Russians that makes them name more blues more than other people?

Try to link what people are like to certain words and expressions for obviously cultural features in their language and you'll find plenty. No one would ever have thought otherwise. But try to link what people are like to how their languages work in a more general sense, along the lines of Whorf's "unperceived intricate systematizations" such as whether they classify things according to shape or material or whether they have a future tense, and all you get is false leads and just-so stories. It seems so tempting and you keep reaching for it, but always and forever, poof and it's gone. It's like trying to get hold of a soap bubble.

The variety among the world's languages in terms of how they work is unrelated to the variety among the world's peoples, and thus Whorfianism cannot be saved even by fashioning a dynamic two-way relationship between cultures and the languages that they are spoken in. That cannot help but seem a strange declaration on first glance, but in this chapter I will demonstrate its empirical motivation.

Rules of the Rain Forest?

Evidential Markers

An eminently tempting case for linking how a language works and what its speakers are like is something that is interesting about another language of the Amazon called Tuyuca. In this language, to make a normal statement you have to include how you know that it's true, or whether you do. This is so deeply entrenched in how you express yourself in Tuyuca that the way you explain how you know something is not with a phrase like "I heard" or "so they say," but with certain suffixes that you tack on to sentences. This is similar to the way we're used to doing it in English to make the past tense (*-ed*) or the plural (*-s*).

So, one does not, as a proper Tuyuca, say just *He's chopping trees*. You have to add one of those suffixes. I am showing the suffixes appended to the English version of the sentence for the sake of clarity—obviously, it is rare that a Tuyuca chooses to express herself in English!

He is chopping trees-**gí** (... I hear.)

He is chopping trees-**í** (... I see.)

He is chopping trees-**hɔ̀i** (... apparently, but I can't tell for sure.)

He is chopping trees-**yigï** (... they say.)

And that's just a sample. There are different versions of the suffixes for the past tense, for whether you are referring to a man, a woman, the person you're talking to, yourself, and so on.

Linguists call these *evidential markers*. Any language has ways of doing what evidential markers do to an extent. In English, when we say after the doorbell rings *That must be the Indian food*, the *must* means roughly the same thing as the Tuyuca suffix used to indicate that you know something because of hearing it. However, Tuyuca takes this kind of thing to an extreme.

Here is where the "holistic" kind of approach may beckon. On the one hand, the previous chapter may have conditioned a skepticism about the classic Whorfian response to data like this. We might resist the idea that having evidential markers makes people magically sensitive to where information came from. Science would be behind us on that. Anna Papafragou at the University of Delaware and her colleagues have shown that Korean children, although having learned the evidential markers in Korean, are no better than English-speaking children at thinking about sources of information.

Yet there may remain a temptation to assume that there must be something about being Tuyuca that conditions this close attention to sources of information: that the culture is feeding into the language. One could suppose it must have something to do with living in a rain forest where one must always be on the alert to dangerous animals, or to the presence of other animals on which one depends for sustenance. Wouldn't being a Tuyuca seem to require constant attention to whether one hears something, whether one can depend on someone's statement that there is a new source of a certain food somewhere far off, and so on?

This sounds eminently plausible when we think only of the Tuyuca. However, as odd as evidential markers seem to an English speaker, they are actually quite common worldwide. Crucially, to perceive any kind of link between culture and evidential markers from a worldwide perspective is—and this is putting it the most open-mindedly—extremely difficult.

Basically, to link evidential markers to what a people are like is to say that some groups are more skeptical than others. However, that is a dicier proposition than it may seem. Evidential markers are rare in Europe, for example, which is much of why they seem so exotic to us. However, who among us is prepared to say that the Ancient Greeks, who produced some of the world's first philosophical treatises scrupulously examining all propositions no matter how basic, and lived in a society always under siege from other empires as well as from rival Greeks themselves, were a relatively accepting, unskeptical people with only a modest interest in sources of information?

Or, I might venture: if you know any Greeks today, would you process them as *not* especially skeptical? I, for one, would say no. Yet Greek has no evidential markers along the lines of Tuyuca. It never has, doesn't, and shows no signs of ever doing so. That's true even though if it did, certainly many would readily link the evidential markers to the grand old Socratic tradition and its influence on Greek thought.

Or, if the Tuyuca have evidential markers because their culture requires them, then why in the world is the only European language that has anything like them Bulgarian? I happen to know some Bulgarians, and I would say that they are pretty skeptical as people go—but no more so than people from many other countries. What is it that Bulgarians have in common culturally with the Tuyuca tribespeople? And more to the point, what do they have in common with Tuyuca tribespeople that Czechs, Macedonians, and Poles do not? Note: it won't do to say that maybe Bulgarian needed the evidential markers in earlier times when Bulgarians were living closer to the land with less technology. If languages furnish speakers' "needs," then why wouldn't the evidential marking have been let go long ago once Bulgarians had central heating and canned food and no longer "needed" them?

Languages evolve according to the needs of their speakers: savor that sentence, but then venture to ask how that squares with Bulgarians being the only Europeans who "needed" evidential markers. Really: why would, say, the traditionally philosophic French, ever defending their geopolitical position, not "need" evidential markers? But no, only Bulgarian—just Bulgarian!— evolved according to that "need"?

Move eastward and another language with evidential marking is Turkish. Again, why them in particular, if evidential marking has anything to do with culture? I have actually encountered a Westerner who had spent some years in Turkey who happily—but with a certain insistence—assumed that it was because Turks were hypersensitive to sources of information. However, he had come to that conclusion based on the evidential marking in the language, not on having independently noted that Turks were hard to convince of anything. Are Turks really more wary of sources of information than, say, Persians? The idea will ring a bell with few if any who are familiar with people of both extractions, and no anthropological study I am aware of makes such an observation or even designates Turks as defined by an extreme wariness of rumor. In fact, if anything, it is Persian culture that is known explicitly as particularly skeptical. But Persian doesn't have evidential markers.

The facts on where we find evidential markers even suggest that seeing them as cultural disrespects an alarmingly vast number of the world's peoples. Basically, skepticism is a form of intelligence. It is certainly a keystone of sophisticated thought. It would not be inappropriate to even state, for general purposes, that skepticism—that is, a dedication to applying one's mind to taking the measure of things before coming to a judgment—is the heart of intelligence. So: on the one hand, we celebrate the Tuyucas' evidential markers as indicating their diligent skepticism. But then, something confronts us: evidential markers are all but unheard of in Africa or Polynesia.

We must restate that gorgeous proposition here: *Languages evolve according to the needs of their speakers.* But what about that this time, cherishing that proposition means that Africans and Polynesians are *not* hypersensitive to sources of information? They are *not* skeptical. They are apparently not—let's face it, this is where the logic takes us—terribly bright. We gifted the Tuyuca with intelligence but must deny it to Africans and Polynesians. Note that this requires harboring such an idea despite how many Africans and Polynesians live in intensely challenging environments, living lives quite similar to those of the Tuyuca. But it would seem that at the end of the day, the Tuyuca rose to the challenge with evidential markers while Africans and Polynesians just shrugged and hoped for the best.

Few will desire to rest there, and as such, we might open up to supposing that evidential markers are less linked to culture than it might seem when we encounter them in one group like the Tuyuca. Evidence for that perspective in fact abounds. If evidential markers emerge according to the "needs" of languages' speakers, then why are they common in the Native American languages of western North America but not the ones in the east? Is it really true that Native Americans living in the Bay Area—not exactly the most rigorously demanding environment—"needed" to be more hypervigilant to sources of information than the ones the Pilgrims endured in those long, frigid winters in the Northeast? ("Squanto *says* there are blackberries still growing three miles that way...")

Plus, the world over, one language will have evidential markers while the one next door, spoken by people living under the same circumstances, will not. In Australia an Aboriginal language called Kayardild has evidential markers—but if they emerged because its speakers "needed" them, then why did the Yukulta language right across the water not have evidential markers? (Yukulta is now extinct, but it was described while some of its speakers were still alive.) The Yukulta lived the same life as the Kayardild, and in fact their languages were basically variations on a single language, in the way that Swedish and Norwegian are.

Evidence of this kind goes on and on. Despite the initial plausibility of thinking Tuyuca has evidential markers because its speakers have a specific need for them, when we pull back the lens, it is clear that evidential markers are not distributed according to what cultures are like. In fact, there is a coherent explanation for where we find evidential markers and where we don't. However, that explanation is not based on cultural needs. The explanation is, quite simply, chance.

The Irrelevance of Necessity

The evidence suggests that evidential markers also tend to spread from one language to another as a kind of grammatical meme carried by bilinguals, in which case the markers are blithely scattered across a wide range of cultures quite unconnected to how vigilant any given one of them is about scuttlebutt and animal noises. This is, essentially, another rendition of chance.

There is a comfort in this reality. At the end of the day, how much of a compliment is it when a Westerner praises a group of people for being skeptical? There is a certain condescension in it, a hair's breadth from "Good show, you all are as bright as us!" A writer I shall not name praises a Third World people on the acknowledgments page of a book for, among other things, being witty and "irreverent"—that is, what goes often under the name "skepticism." But why wouldn't they be witty and irreverent? Which Homo sapiens aren't? The passage is deeply condescending. And yet, for whatever it's worth, the language of the people has no evidential markers!

However, it does have definite and indefinite articles, words for *the* and *a*. Those little words allow a language's speakers to distinguish something already mentioned (*the* fact that some languages have evidential markers) from something new to the exchange (*a* related point about definite and indefinite articles). Maybe we can save this particular unskeptical group by celebrating its intelligent distinction of the definite from the indefinite? Not really, because overall, having words for *the* and *a*, as utterly normal as it feels to an English speaker, is something of a European kink. East of, roughly, the Baltic and the Balkans you don't find much *the* and *a*.

As such, if *the* and *a* are based on speakers' needs, then we have to say that Western Europeans are more given than most of the world's peoples to distinguishing things already mentioned from things just brought up. Not only would this make little sense and even seem a tad arrogant, but there are microcosmic problems as well. Pity the ethnographer charged to determine why Finns have no "need" to distinguish *the* and *a* whereas the Dutch do. Plus, even if we could cobble together a solution to these conundrums (Finns are more reserved than the Dutch, and so they don't need to … be as … specific … ??) the reality of things throws us another curve ball. Having words for *the* and *a* is otherwise common in a strip of languages across the middle of Africa. Not the West Coast or the southern segment, mind you, but a band across the middle, composed of people with decidedly little in common with people in Barcelona or Copenhagen and in fact having had, historically, vastly little contact with them. Once again, the explanation here is not culture but chance.

Worldwide, chance is, itself, the only real pattern evident in the link between languages and what their speakers are like. As often as not, what seem like possible links end up not being what we would expect and would be highly unlikely to motivate a study. A key example is cases that force us into supposing that people *don't* "need" something that they nevertheless clearly have, and that all people do. In New Guinea, for instance, it is quite common for a language to have one word that covers both *eat* and *drink* (and sometimes also *smoke*). Yet what "need" does this address? It is unlikely that anyone would propose that dozens of separate tribes on this massive island are actively uninterested in the differences between foods ("How many times do I have to tell you to *stop calling attention* to the fact that fruit is different from stew??"). Descriptions of such groups' take on food in fact regularly include a wide variety of foodstuffs and preparations, with feasting as a regular aspect of communal life.

This then sheds light on what we might make of a superficially more auspicious situation. Navajo takes things to the opposite extreme: how you say *eat* depends on whether you are just eating in general or whether what you are eating is hard, soft, stringy, round, a bunch of little things, or meat. Future research could determine how the place of food differs in Native American cultures versus ones in New Guinea? Perhaps, but what do we make of the fact that an Aboriginal group across the water from New Guinea in Queensland, the Dyirbal, having lived lives over millennia that New Guineans would find thoroughly familiar, have three different *eat* verbs for eating fish, meat, and vegetables? Or that an Amazonian group called the Jarawara, living lives also quite like those of New Guinea folk, say *eat* differently depending on whether you have to chew something a lot or a little, whether you have to spit out its seeds, or whether you have to suck on it?

All of this is neat, but not in showing us anything about what people need in their language. A speculation about how something in a language "must" reflect something essential in its speakers is incomplete without considering the distribution of that something in languages worldwide.

★ ★ ★

The truth about how languages are different is that largely they differ in the degree to which they do the same things. Some take a trait further than others, not because their speakers "needed" it to, but because a bubble happened to pop up somewhere in the soup. In English, one bubble was the emergence of *the*. It was basically a matter of the word *that* going viral. *That* singles something out—*Not that cat, the other one. The* is the child of *that*: it's what happened when *that* wore down. The wearing down meant that the word is shorter, for one, and then also that the meaning is less explicit: *the* throws a dim but useful little light on something—*I meant the green one, not just any old crayon*. English, then, is particular in marking definiteness even when context would have done the job just as well. New words emerge this way all the time: *a* and *an* started as *one*.

Yet we have seen that the birth of *the* cannot have been a cultural event. Bubbles generally aren't. There is simply no reason we could identify that a word like *that* wore down into the word *the* so often in the western half of a peninsula called Europe, in a band running across the middle of Africa, but much less anywhere else. Crucially, no language leaves definiteness completely to context; it's just that English happened to take that particular ball and run with it. Many languages use good old *that* (and *this*) to mark definiteness when explicitly needed. Chinese does it with word order: *Train arrived* means *the* train came, while if you say *Arrived train* it means that *a* train came. Languages all accomplish the same things despite how massively different human cultures are. It happens, however, that each language happens to develop its random private obsessions, rather like a little fellow who can name all of the presidents' wives for no real reason (that was me as a lad).

Evidential markers are examples; they emerge via the same kind of process as words like *the* and *a*. They seem so "cultural" from our vantage point, but then *the* and *a* would seem just as "cultural" to a Tuyuca. Both traits are bubbles in the soup. All languages mark evidentiality to some degree. English's *That must be the Indian food* is paralleled by Spanish doing it with the future tense (*Será Juan* "That must be John"). It's just that some languages happen to take that ball and run with it. Meanwhile, all people eat, drink, and like it. Some languages happen to bubble up a bouquet of words for different kinds of eating, some just bubble up with a word for *eat* and a word for *drink*, while some don't even bubble in this area at all and just leave it at a single word for taking things into your mouth.

It is the nature of language for such bubbles to pop up. All languages are on the boil; none sit unheated. The only question is where a language's bubbles will happen to occur. It's exciting, actually—examining this language and that one, there is almost a suspense as to which intriguing feature will turn up in which one. Another way of seeing it is as a kind of extravagance. In any language, there are some things that it elevates to an art, sashaying rather than walking, performing instead of just going through the motions. "What will the fashions be next year?," one might wonder—and in the same way you wonder what marvelous predilection the next language you encounter will happen to flaunt. Yet, unexpected as this may seem, these predilections do not track with culture. It's more like someone opting to sport a certain scarf for one season just "because," and maybe developing a penchant for a certain color for a while some years later. Serendipity plays a much vaster role in language than one would expect.

Nothing makes that clearer than the fact that many of the things we think of as absolutely fundamental to getting our thoughts across are, in grand view, more bubbles. There are languages, for example, where you do not have to mark tense at all—no past, no future. Context takes care of everything, and yet the people live life as richly as we do. What that means is that even having tense is, technically, a pretty scarf, a bauble—or bubble. After all, if most of the world's languages developed tense because they "needed" it, then we must say that various peoples did not "need" to know whether something happened before or hasn't happened yet. But what kind of people would these be? Who would be comfortable smiling at them and telling them that unlike us, they don't need to situate themselves in time? Never mind that the people are in New Guinea—last time we checked, someone was already accusing them of not being gourmands!

Or, there are languages where there are simply first-, second-, and third-person pronouns, but no difference between singular and plural among any of them. We're used to this in English with *you* applying to both one and more than one person (and that is odder, as languages go, than we are often aware). However, imagine if *he, she, it,* and *they* were the same word, and *I* and *we* were the same word. There are people who don't have to imagine that, because that's the way their languages are! However, it would be hard to tell them that they do not "need" to distinguish between *he* and *they*. For what reasons would a group of human beings "not need" to make that distinction? This time the Pirahã are among those whom we would have to designate as having such peculiarly sparse needs. This just in: "Tribe with No Words for *We, They,* or *Y'all* Cannot Distinguish Groups from Individuals"? Rather, most of the world's languages, including English, make the distinction because all languages have bubbles. Context is capable of taking care of a great deal. All languages express much, much more than anything any human beings "need."

* * *

Once we understand this, it is no longer surprising that languages seem almost willful in how little their makeup has to do with what its speakers are like. It's all about the bubbles. The Nunamiut and Tareumiut Eskimo have distinctly different cultures: the Nunamiut are hunters living in family groups while the Tareumiut are whalers living in big villages. Yet they speak the exact same language. Another one: when *t* or *d* come at the end of a word and after another consonant, we often let it go when speaking casually. We are much more likely to say *Wes' Side Story* than *Wes-t Side Story*. Someone may well say *I tol' Allen not to* rather than *I tol-d Allen not to*. This is true of all English speakers to varying extents. However, as it happens, before a pause in speaking, New Yorkers are more likely to drop *t*'s and *d*'s than people an hour-and-change down the road in Philadelphia! That is, if *You're gonna catch a cold* is the last thing someone says before quieting down for a while, it's more likely to come out as *You're gonna catch a col'* in New York than in Philadelphia.

Try to wrap your head around what this would mean culturally—are Philadelphians more properly spoken than New Yorkers? Note that the study that discovered this focused on ordinary people, not the hypereducated elite. Our question is therefore whether the people in the *Rocky* movies are more careful about pronunciation than the people in *Saturday Night Fever*. Plus, we mean only in that quirkily specific case, before a pause. In general both New Yorkers and Philadelphians drop their *t*'s and *d*'s all over the place just like anyone else—although in other subtly differing ways that no speaker could ever be aware of consciously. It's all about bubbles again.

Why would a language have something its speakers don't need? We can see now why the question, so reasonable in itself, misses something about language that only becomes evident in view of all of them at a time: most of a language's workings are not due to need, but happenstance. Whorf's idea about "intricate systematizations" was that to learn a language's grammar was to learn how its speakers think, how they are: master Tibetan's grammatical patterns and you are mastering, as it were, Tibetanness. This is a plausible place to start when thinking about language, but less attractive as a place to remain. Tuyuca speakers no more "need" evidential markers than Western European and Central African persons "need" words for *the* and *a*. Traits like this in a language do not emerge because of the way its speakers think, upon which there is also no motivation to suppose that these linguistic traits consequently shape speakers' cultural essence. As tempting as this latter "holistic" approach is, while it allows the viscerally attractive idea that the Tuyuca are uniquely attuned to their environment, it also requires that millions of people in New Guinea don't care about good eating.

Not *Those* Things?

There could be a sense that the traits that are rather obviously unamenable to any cultural analysis are not the ones Whorfianism applies to. However, it is unclear why they would not be. If referring to time with the words *up* and *down* makes Chinese people process life in a significantly different way than English speakers, then why *doesn't* a single word for *eat*, *drink*, and *smoke* mean that people in New Guinea process ingestion differently than other people? One can even imagine ethno-centric Victorians cooking up—so to speak—an idea that these New Guinea verbs signal the primitive palates we would expect of "savages." We dismiss that easily—but upon what grounds would people's languages correspond to their cultures only in attractive ways? Upon which grounds would we even decide what, in the grand scheme of things, is immutably attractive?

Sheer logic forces a simple conclusion: the idea that Amazonians have evidential markers because they need to be alert to their environment is every bit as much a just-so story as one that New Guineans have an eat-drink verb because they can't be bothered to savor their dinner.

"No Word for X": Caveat Lector

One hears now and then of things about some language that suggest an actual robust correspondence with its speakers' take on life, but in my experience they always turn out to be myths.

There are, to be sure, countless things that any language does not have a single word for that clearly do not reflect anything its speakers are or feel. The French person might wonder whether there were people who *don't* have a word for the kind of person who always seems to be a little cold like their word *frilleux*. Yet English doesn't—we have to say, indeed, "I'm always cold." Yet few would propose that this is because the French are more sensitive to breezes than others. Clearly, that the French have a word *frilleux* and we don't is just a jolly little accident, as is the fact that Swedish happens not to have a word for *wipe*. Let's not even imagine telling Swedes they don't wipe—it's just that they use words like *dry* and *erase*, which serve just as well.

The propositions that really would suggest a different take on life always fall apart. The film *Amistad* taught us that the African language Mende has no word for *may*. The idea was to highlight the basic innocence of one of the African characters, his language supposedly requiring one to specify whether something is or isn't, with no gray zones. It was great narrative drama, but cartoon linguistics. It is safe to say that no language lacks ways of conveying degrees of confidence in truth, given that all humans have the cognitive equipment for perceiving such gradation and urgently need to express it day in and day out. Mende, in fact, has a much more robust and elaborate subjunctive construction than English does. In that language, one not only does and doesn't, but may and may not.

The Language Log website's "No Word for X" department is a useful archive of how things like this never pan out. I have also heard that a dialect of Berber, spoken in northern Africa by people who were living there on the land long before Arabic got there, has no words for *win* or *lose*. We are supposed to think of them as in contact with the communal, cooperative essence that we acquisitive individualists in the West have fallen for. There is value in the lesson, but it would be more honestly conveyed by addressing what the Shilha Berbers are like as a culture, not their language. Anthropology tells us that all human groups have games, especially among children. Are the Berber really alien to children engaging in scrappy competitions in which one person comes out the victor and one doesn't? If not, then right there, we know that these are not a people with no concept of winning and losing; the queston becomes whether they watch winning and losing happening all the time and yet mysteriously lack a word for it. This would seem highly implausible, not to mention condescending.

And then, a dictionary of precisely the Shilha's dialect of Berber reveals words for *win* and *lose*. Perhaps they do not use the words just as we do, indeed—especially since the dictionary is in French and *gagner* and *perdre* themselves overlap only partially with English's *win* and *lose*. However, the same dictionary also had words for *conquer* and *fail*. Plus, as it happened, I once had a Berber-speaking cab driver, and when I asked him how to say *win* and *lose* he immediately tossed out exactly the two words for them I had seen in the dictionary! Let's face it, these people not only know what winning and losing are, but talk about them with ease.

Who Thinks Otherwise?

Some readers may understandably wonder whether there are actually people informed about languages and cultures who would find anything I am putting forth at all novel. There are: how one perceives such things varies immensely depending on training, cultural predilections, and intent, and a robust strain in modern academia is quite committed to the idea that languages represent cultural thought patterns. For example, Swarthmore's K. David Harrison has posited that depicting language diversity as marvelously random, as I have, is "stunningly obtuse." He happens to have done so in a passing critique of an article I wrote in *World Affairs*. That personal aspect, however, is not my reason for using his position as an example here. For instance, his claim that I think language's complexities render them unfit for the modern world and that it would be better if all people were monolingual are so contrary to anything I have ever written that the proper response is silence.

However, Harrison's take on the link between language and culture is useful to the argument here in demonstrating exactly the unwitting misimpressions I have described in this chapter. When it comes to grammar, as opposed to what they have names for, languages are awesomely different, but not in ways that correspond to how peoples are different. Harrison disagrees: "If so, then Stonehenge and Machu Picchu differ only because of different randomly evolved building methods, but tell us nothing interesting about the ancient Neolithic and fourteenth-century Inca cultures."

But that's just it—languages are not things. Stonehenge and Machu Picchu, as tokens of culture, tell us plenty about the people who built them. However, if we had records of the language Stonehenge's builders spoke, its structure could tell us nothing about what they were like, nor would early Quechua teach us anything about what it was to be an Inca in the 1500s. Both languages, of course, had words for things important in their cultures. However, from where the idea that what shapes thought is the word for something rather than the thing itself?

Harrison continues to protest against the idea that language changes randomly: "It's hard to imagine a lesser regard for the products of human genius and their great diversity that arises differently under different conditions. As people have spread out and populated the planet, they have continually adapted, applying their ingenuity to solve unique survival problems in each location, and inventing unique ways of conceptualizing ideas. Geographic isolation and the struggle for survival have been the catalyst for immense creativity."

But languages are not like paintings. They do not develop via people applying their ingenuity or being creative. Languages develop via step-by-step driftings that operate below the level of consciousness, and this is not an opinion, but a fact, fundamental to any introductory class on language change. How else, after all, did Estonian end up with fourteen cases?

nominative	raamat	"book"
genitive	raamat-u	"of the book"
partitive	raamat-u-t	"some book"
illative	raamatu-sse	"into the book"
inessive	raamatu-s	"in the book"
elative	raamatu-st	"out of the book"
allative	raamatu-le	"onto the book"
adessive	raamatu-l	"on the book"
ablative	raamatu-lt	"off from the book"
translative	raamatu-ks	"like a book"
terminative	raamatu-ni	"as far as the book"
essive	raamatu-na	"as a book"
abessive	raamatu-ta	"without the book"
comitative	raamatu-ga	"with the book"

On top of all of that, Estonian is one of those languages where irregularity is practically the rule. Does anyone plan such things? If this is creativity, I'm not sure we're giving Estonians a compliment.

The impression that people "create" their grammars is easily maintained when we marvel at a language unlike ours spoken by indigenous people. When a language works so differently from ours, a natural gut-level impression is that it is a departure from normality, and even that this departure must have been deliberately effected, or must have arisen because of some pressing circumstance such as interesting cultural particularities. However, the notion falls apart when we turn the lens on ourselves. Spanish has subjunctive endings. Who "created" them? In what way do they correspond to life in Madrid as opposed to life in Tokyo? If we are to say that they are historical baggage from another time, why was a subjunctive more useful in Old Castile—or Ancient Rome, where Spanish's ancestor Latin already had a subjunctive—than in feudal Japan?

Or, if we are to say that the Whorfian analysis isn't supposed to apply to the subjunctive, why not? It is not clear from Whorfian work to date what would disqualify the subjunctive from the analysis while permitting numeral classifiers, color terms, and the future tense. After all, if European languages didn't have the subjunctive and we encountered it instead in a tiny language spoken in a rain forest, wouldn't it be the first thing treated as evidence of its speakers' layered perspective on truth conditions?

* * *

The magnificence of how a language is built is not its correspondence with folkways, cosmology, and thought patterns,
but in its protean, fecund independence from these things, ever
happening to burgeon into new spaces of meaning and complexity, evidencing what one can barely help thinking of as a
kind of irrepressibility. To think of the most interesting thing
about language as being how it sheds light on its speakers'
thought processes is like cherishing Beethoven's Seventh Sym-
phony not for its nimble melodies, richness of harmony, surg-
ing thematic progressions, and stirring orchestration, but for
the handful of dimly flickering hints that it just might lend us
about what Beethoven was like as a dude.

In the synaesthetic sense, a language smells like mowed
grass or a steamy jungle. It cooks—bubbles, as it were. However, it does not do this on assignment from a culture's needs.
Like culture, but largely apart from it, language is quite the
marvel in itself.

CHAPTER 3

An Interregnum
On Culture

IT CAN BE SURPRISING to see how weak the connection is between language structure and people. Readers may justifiably sense an implication at this point in my argumentation that language has nothing to do with culture, or at least nothing important or interesting.

Nothing could be further from the truth, and before I proceed with my case, I must make clear that I am referring solely to a *particular* argument about language and culture, rather than, say, dismissing the entire field of linguistic anthropology.

Whorfianism versus Words

Especially intuitive to all of us is that words and expressions in our language can be cultural. A reader might ask, for example, "How can he mean that *Insha'Allah* [God willing] isn't an integral part of expressing oneself as a Muslim?"

I say: yes, these things are linguistic renditions of culture. Cultures are lived by human beings; human beings have language; hence, language will have words and expressions for aspects of culture. If language and culture never intersected, our job would be to explore why in the world—*why, ever* in the world—they did not.

Culture can even, in a direct and obvious way, require expression through grammar as well as words. Geography is the usual example. As we have seen, a culture that takes place on flat terrain will mean that Guugu Yimithirr speakers say "north of me" instead of "in front of me," while a culture in a mountainous region like the Tzeltal might say "uphill" rather than "left."

Good: my question is not whether language and culture intersect. They can (although only *can*: the Tzotzil living in the same mountainous environment still say "left" just like someone in Detroit). However, my interest is in Whorfianism, which is something quite different from words for things front and center, such as objects, concepts, and topographies. The Whorfian claim is about more than whether languages have *terms* for what things and surroundings their speakers think about.

Whorfianism claims that languages make their speakers think *in* a certain way—with language not just giving labels to particular things and concepts in the culture, but making people think in certain overarching patterns, such as processing time as up and down rather than across, or feeling, eating, and drinking as the same action. My question, like Whorfianism's, is about language on the level beyond the basic one of affixing labels to persons, places, things, practices. The focus is on how a language's grammar works, its random particularities in vocabulary like distinguishing dark blue from light blue, its not happening to have a future tense, or its having the articles *the* and *a*, which is hard for, say, Russians (whose language has no *the* or *a*) to learn in English.

That is, Whorfianism is not about the things a language's speakers immediately think of as particular in their language—"We say *Insha'Allah*," "We live near a mountain"—but the things they dismiss with a shrug that turn out to be quite unusual in comparison to languages they have no reason to know much about. That is, the kind of things that made Whorf's ideas novel and still attended to decades later. The Tuyucan, for instance, might ask, "Are there people who *don't* have to utter a suffix showing how they know anything they mention?"

Do *these* things—Whorf's "intricate systematizations"—mean that a language's speakers see the world in a unique way? When a Muslim person says *Insha'Allah* it is certainly an expression of her culture, a label for an orientation integral to Islam—but the question is whether there is anything about Arabic as a grammatical or vocabulary *system* that parallels the Muslim soul, in a holistic sense, beyond that of simple labels for things and concepts. I salute anyone who masters Arabic. Yet how much of what they tore themselves up to get a handle on, such as the verb endings, the gender, the definite articles, the guttural sounds—how much of that, not just expressions like *Insha'Allah*—was a matter of getting a sense of how Muslims think?

Essentially, none. They mastered a grammatical conglomeration that happened to come out the way it did—one language out of the six thousand variations on a theme that the world's languages are.

There Are Words and There Are Words

The intersection between language and culture, however, goes deeper than the plain-vanilla fact that languages have words for things their speakers consider important. For example, the aforementioned is actually but one symptom of a broader, less obvious, and therefore more engrossing aspect of language: what is often termed *ethnosemantics*. Ethnosemantics explores how languages' usage of a word or group of words, which on the surface seem as if they would have the same meanings for all people everywhere, differ according to the worldview of the language's speakers.

Surely, then, the fact that the Chinese have been using the formal *you* pronoun *nín* with more frequency since the 1980s is connected to something cultural, namely the social transformation as Communism gives ever more space to capitalism, which soft pedals the Communist focus on egalitarianism in favor of more traditional modes of hierarchical deference. Few would dissociate, either, that very strain of millennia-old deference in the culture from the fact that Mandarin has distinct words for elder versus younger brother (or sister).

Whorfianism, in this light, can be seen as an attempt to expand the ethnosemantic perspective beyond intuitive and immediately demonstrable cases like the Mandarin ones, and it is this expansion that my manifesto questions. To trace an increase in the usage of a formal *you* word to a growing fashion for formality is one thing. To trace an absence of a word for blue to seeing the sky as less blue than English speakers do is another thing—and, although those making that claim do not have occasion to consider—akin to tracing obscure groups' lack of separate words for *eat* and *drink* to being less alive to the gastronomic pleasures than we are.

Whorfianism, that is, proposes that the ethnosemantic perspective applies beyond the obvious. I, on the contrary, argue that it applies exactly where basic intuition would place it but no further. In no way, however, does that dismiss the richness of actual ethnosemantic investigations.

What's with Stand-up Comedy?

Another way that language and culture intersect, one I find especially illuminating for addressing human differences in a systematic way, is in an approach called *ethnography of communication*. In all human groups there is a certain set of fundamental aspects of how language is used.

Described in the abstract they seem rather obvious, and even dull. For example: using language might involve one, two, three, or many more persons. Using language might take place at a sermon, or a wedding, or in a casual conversation. Language might involve various goals: a bargain, some amusement, an argument, seduction. Language might involve statements, questions, or quotations. Language might be solemn or jocular. Language might come in a continuous stream, or occur between long pauses, or be delivered right up close to your face. Language might be delivered orally or on paper or in some other way.

Yes, by itself this hardly seems a grand insight. However, when human language is viewed according to this toolkit (all of the above alternate possibilities have specific terminological designations, and there are some more of them), seemingly "weird" practices worldwide become utterly, diversely, normal.

In Panama, for instance, every other day the Kuna listen to a two-hour speech by their chief in which he discusses politics, religion, or history. An official responder says "It is so" after each "verse" of the speech. The speech is couched in a highly formal and allusive fashion, after which a spokesman interprets it in clearer terms for the audience. The chief signals that his speech is over by abruptly lowering his voice.

To us this sounds like a "rite." With all due respect for it, we may have a quiet sense that it seems a tad over the top or at least arbitrary. We, for example, do not listen regularly to two-hour speeches about "the way it is." However, Americans very much did up through the nineteenth century—Lincoln's Gettysburg Address was a sidebar in an event whose focus was orator Edward Everett speaking grandly for two hours about, very much, "the way it is." Americans were more like the Kuna back then, although they wouldn't have thought of it that way.

But more to the point, even today the difference between Americans and the Kuna in terms of that sermon is merely one of what is called *instrumentality* in ethnography of communication terminology. The Kuna get frequent doses of commentary delivered orally—but many of us get at least an hour's worth of commentary about "the way it is" daily via the radio, the television, or the Internet. What differs is the medium, the *instrumentality*, not the substance.

The Kuna chief speaks in an artificially elevated register—but then so many of us receive religious teachings in one as well, only written on the page—again, in a different *instrumentality*. The chief's speech register differs from ordinary Kuna in a fashion similar to how the English of the St. James Bible differs from colloquial modern English. Cultures differ in where they situate high language as opposed to casual speech—what ethnography of communication work terms rather opaquely a different *act sequence*—but not in whether they have it.

The Kuna have their interlocutor explain the language. Many of us will recognize this from Sunday school, but it also applies to the function of the Sunday service itself, or to the extent that the event was about "the way it is," a schoolteacher or college professor getting across what scholars have discovered. Or, how weird that the Kuna chief lowers his voice to show that the speech is over—but when a football game gets exciting a sports announcer slides into saying everything on a higher pitch and concludes with strangely elongated vowels ("and here it goes . . . ARLINGTON GOES FOR IT, HE GETS RIGHT PAST PATTERSON, HE'S OFF LIKE A SHOT, IT'S ALL OVER, ARLINGTON SCORES THE TOUCHDOWN AND THAT'S THE GAAAME, TWENTY-ONE SEVEN . . ."). Think about it—the announcer isn't *in* the game to get this vocally heated up, and microphone technology absolves him of any need to raise his voice or elongate his vowels like Edward Everett had to. Yet an announcer who auditioned by just quietly describing what he was seeing would never be hired: a sports announcer must master, in a performative sense, a certain *manner*, in ethnography of communication terminology, just as the Kuna chief must.

And as for the Kuna responder repeatedly interjecting "It is so," how odd is this compared to, say, Ed McMahon? The late-night talk show "sidekick" is different from the Kuna "responder" only in which *event*, in ethnography of communication terminology, he works at—a broadcast performance versus a speech. Really, they are not all that different.

To the Kuna, utterly "ritual" would be the American practice of stand-up comedy, where a person is paid a fee to stand up before an assemblage of people and recite to them comments carefully composed to make their diaphragms titter with laughter for twenty minutes, and then thanks them for laughing and walks off the stage. This is as peculiar and coded a practice as any tribal one we might see on the Discovery Channel and is based on a fragile web of expectations as to speech style, response, and performativity.

Certainly, that we find stand-up comedy so ordinary is an interesting intersection of language and culture, which the ethnography of communication paradigm makes sense of. One will find a similar approach called *semiotic functionalism* as another way in which we could never understand how language was being used without framing it as a cultural variation.

Culture Shaping Grammar: It Happens

There is even a way in which culture correlates with what languages are like structurally, as opposed to how they are used. Languages spoken by small indigenous groups tend to be more grammatically complex than widely spoken ones and are more likely to have the odder, harder to produce sounds like the famous clicks of a family of languages spoken by the Khoi-San hunter-gatherers in southern Africa. This surprises most people. One might expect that complex grammar would be more typical of "advanced" civilizations. Anthropologists and sociologically oriented linguists often remark that they would expect that intimate groups would have less need of the precision of things like gender and elaborate verb tenses, because shared context could compensate for the fragmentation and impersonality of urban life.

The reason languages with fewer speakers are more complicated is not because the complexity befits their speakers in some way, but because for a language to be spoken by massive numbers of people tends to mean that it was imposed on nonnative speakers at some point, and therefore beaten up by the mundane fact that it's tough to really learn a language after adolescence.

In other words, the complex kind of language is a norm—it's the way almost every language on earth has become over countless millennia of stepwise accretions of "mess." First a feminine gender marker, then a subjunctive mood, next some evidentials, later a language becomes tonal—one never knows just what will happen, but something will, and then something else, and then something else. After a while you have the awesome mess that is a language. The only thing that interferes with this norm is the odd circumstance of people learning a language as adults rather than as children— something that has happened mostly in recent millennia as technology has allowed vast and rapid population movements.

Thus it's the more streamlined languages that are the departures. It's not an accident that English has no grammatical gender of the Spanish *el sombrero* "the hat"/*la luna* "the moon" sort and rather feeble verb conjugation consisting largely of scattered -*s* and -*ed*. When Scandinavian Vikings invaded England starting in the eighth century, they learned Old English, a vastly more complicated language than modern English, about as well as the typical American learns French or Spanish. There were so many of them, marrying English women, that their children heard their version of Old English as much as native Old English. In the absence of media or widespread literacy, after a while the Vikings' way of speaking transformed what English was.

Within the context of this book, however, we should notice that while this is indeed an example of culture shaping grammar, the process does not hinge on "needs" specific to particular cultures. That English is relatively streamlined as languages go is not because something about being an English speaker requires one to be less precise than a herdsman speaking an obscure language in Siberia, but because of something quite brutal that befell it in its history. "Needs" were relevant only in the sense that adults under such circumstances "need" to communicate as best they can, which is different from "needing" *not* to have gender or a pluperfect.

The facts are similar for Mandarin Chinese, Persian, Swahili, Indonesian, and other curiously adult-friendly languages worldwide. Conversely, languages like the click languages, Navajo with its universally irregular verbs, or Yélî Dnye with its thousands of prefixes and suffixes are not complex because their speakers need them to be that way, but because that level of complexity—massively surpassing what humans need for communication—is what all languages are normally like. This means, however, that languages like English result from a cultural impact, in a broad sense, on how a grammar is built.

Language and Universals: A Clarification

I hope to have made it clear that I, like most investigators of language, feel that an academic culture that treated language entirely apart from the cultures of the people that speak them would be not only arid but empirically hopeless.

For example, in the message that languages show the universal in humanity, some spontaneously hear a shout-out to Noam Chomsky's proposal about an innate "universal grammar" that all languages share. That theory, now subscribed to by a worldwide community of practicing syntacticians, sees language as based on a conglomeration of neurally encoded structures that determine how words are arranged in sentences. Identifying the hypothesized neural structures is beyond science at this point, but Chomskyan syntax attempts to elucidate them via inference, comparing sentence patterns in various languages and modeling them according to abstract algorhythmic schemas of the kind that computer scientists are familiar with.

A fundamental tenet of this enterprise is that all languages are based on a single universal grammar pattern, with their variations due to alternate settings of various "switches." Flip one switch that controls word order in a very specific way and you have the difference between a language that says *You took his book* and *You book his took*. Flip another one to determine whether you have to use subject pronouns or not: *I speak* when it's off and Spanish's *hablo* with no *yo* for *I* when it's on. All a child has to learn is which way her language flips its switches and then plug in the words.

To Chomskyans, then, diversity in languages' grammars is a kind of illusion: they are all the same language underneath, and to study languages awed with their diversity rather than with their underlying likeness is to miss "the point." Less charitable practitioners have even been known to dismiss the study of language from other angles as "not real linguistics," less intellectually rigorous than delving into the densely jargoned tools of Chomkyan syntax.

Predictably, quite a few linguists are otherwise inclined, feeling not only that they deserve the name, but that they consider an approach to language that takes no account of its speakers and what they are like as intellectually barren and even empirically hopeless. To them, language, as a fundamentally social phenomenon, cannot be treated as if it were simply a computer software program. In truth, despite a certain glamour factor surrounding Chomskyan syntacticians— Chomsky's name helps, and in the 1960s when the approach was new and less hermetically abstract than it has since become, it did revolutionize linguistics as a field—most linguists resist its uniquely stringent conception of a queerly complex mental module distinct from all else that cognition comprises.

I count myself among them: my claim that languages' diversity teaches us what we have in common is not an espousal of the conception of universal grammar I have just described. Like most linguists, I believe that there is an innate predisposition to use language. However, a promising hypothesis as to its neural configuration will be compatible with the fundamentals of evolutionary theory and human cognition, in a fashion that Chomskyan syntax does not even make an attempt to be. Moreover, much of my linguistics work is focused on how sociohistorical conditions have affected how languages are structured throughout human history, while some of my work for the media has explored language in modern social context.

Overall, the spontaneous affection for Whorfianism among so many linguists and fellow travelers is partly rooted in a visceral resistance to a certain cultural hegemony that Chomskyan linguistics maintains. One is to question a linguistics that has no room for personhood. I do think that this position itself becomes somewhat reflexive and oversimplified—the study of indigenous cultures, or how people construct their identities through language, will play no role in the discovery of the neural configuration that allows human speech regardless of where one is born. Yet, my manifesto is not a dog-whistle to

Chomskyan conceptions of an abstract universal grammar that models English and Japanese as the same language with a different set of switch flips. How we talk is, certainly, connected to how we are.

Moving Along

As such, there are ways that language intersects with culture beyond those I have discussed here. I take issue with the approaches and conclusions of none of them, and even on the basis of this brief chapter, the case rests: language would seem to have an awful lot to do with culture.

What this book takes issue with is a specific question. Does a language's structure, in terms of what it does with words and how it puts them together, conspire to shape thought to such an extent that we would reasonably term it a "worldview," a perspective on life robustly different from that of someone whose language structures words and grammar differently? Does every language, as Jack Hitt phrased it, have "its unique theology and philosophy" quietly but mind-alteringly "buried in its very sinews"?

Many feel that the answer to that question is yes, but their grounds for that conclusion create as many problems as they solve. I can now explain why, with it clear that I am arguing not that language and culture have no relationship but that they are separate in an aspect highly particular but widely discussed and with significant implications. Let us move on, for example, to China.

CHAPTER 4

Dissing the Chinese

MUCH OF THE APPEAL of Whorfianism is the idea that other people's languages lead them to pay more attention to certain things than English speakers do. Investigators seek to show that certain particularities of a language make people more sensitive to the material of things, to grades of blueness, to the gender that their language happens to assign to inanimate objects. Indeed, many languages are chock full of constructions that call attention to nuances of environment that an English speaker would scarcely imagine any language's grammar would have anything to do with. One duly supposes that all of the bells and whistles in such a language might indicate a kind of hypersensitivity to certain facets of living—that the rest of us ought marvel at and perhaps even take a page from.

The Normal Language: Beyond English Indeed

Part of what got thinkers like Whorf and other specialists in Native American languages into this frame of mind is that those languages tend to be janglingly elaborate in terms of what they pay attention to. The impression from a Native American language is typically that there is so *much* of it—that is, that one must attend to so very many things just to form a basic sentence. Of the languages in the world so full of meticulously particular distinctions that I can't quite wrap my head around the idea of someone speaking them without effort, outside of the Slavic languages, almost all of them are Native American ones. Sitting in on a seminar at Berkeley about Cree years ago, for example, I endlessly remarked to the professor Richard Rhodes that I could not believe anybody could keep track of so many things in a language they actually lived life in—and he knew what I meant and cherished the language for exactly that reason. (It is to him that I owe a great deal for calling attention to the fearsome complexity of indigenous languages.)

The Atsugewi language of California is a great example, extinct as of recently but while it was still spoken, goodness gracious! For example: the sentence for "The soot flowed into the creek" was *W'oq^{h}putíc'ta c^ə ni$^ɂə$ qáp^h c^ə c'uméyi*. Breaking it down into its pieces in all of its forbidding unfamiliarity need not detain us here; suffice it to know that within that one sentence is a magnificent fussiness.

The word for *move* is a specific one used when referring to things like dirt—if it's other things moving you use different words for *move*. The word for *into* is used only if it's liquid being gone "into"; otherwise you use other words for *into* according to the substance (shades of that New Guinea language Yélî Dnye's multiple words for *on*). Never mind that there's already a suffix elsewhere in the sentence that itself means just "to"—it's as if the language somehow thinks that wouldn't be enough. Another suffix tells us that the sentence is factual as opposed to hypothetical, which would seem to be obvious from the fact that the person is saying it, but this language dots its *i*'s and crosses its *t*'s indeed! Then, the *c*ᵊ (pronounced roughly "tsuh") marks the words *soot* and *creek* as nouns—just in case it isn't clear that they are.

There is something delicious in speculating how a language like that might shape the thoughts of its speakers—lots of different words for *move*, *into*-ness being a Hydra-headed thing, getting highly explicit that things are things. To the extent that it might even give an English speaker a touch of an inferiority complex about our less elaborate language, this, too, can feel welcome in its way. Seeing how languages like Atsugewi work is an elegant and conclusive lesson in the mental equality of all human beings.

Whorfianism, here, seems beneficial.

But.

* * *

Languages differ much more than Atsugewi and English in how much they pack into a sentence. English, as languages go, is about in the middle of a scale of telegraphicness. It's easy to suppose that English's degree of complexity is "normal," but a great many languages make English look like Atsugewi.

Let's take a simple and endlessly translated sentence: *In the beginning, God created the heavens and the earth*. In languages that scan the way we are accustomed, that sentence requires attending to certain grammatical processes. In English, the sentence marks the past tense (*created*), has definite articles, and marks the plural (*heavens*). In the original Hebrew, this was *Bereshit bara Elohim et hashamayim ve'et ha'arets*. This, too, had past tense marking in *bara* "created," definite articles (*ha-*), and plural marking (*-im*), as well as marking the heavens and the earth as objects rather than subjects with the *et* particle.

Other languages pack a little more into the sentence. In Russian, it is *B načale sotvoril Bog nebo i zemlju*. There is no definite article in Russian, but we have the past tense, the plural marking, and the marking of earth (*zemlj-u*) as an object with a suffix. In addition, Russian requires that we mark "beginning" with the locative marker *-e* (*načal-e*), and the *so-* in the word *sotvoril* for "created" serves to indicate that the creation happened at one time rather than over a long period.

Other languages utterly unrelated to European or Middle Eastern ones operate on quite a different plan, but maintain about the same level of busyness. In Tagalog, the main language of the Philippines, the sentence is *Nang pasimula ay nilikha ng Diyos ang langit at ang lupa*. The little word *ay* just pops up when you start a sentence with something other than a verb. Never mind why, but it's something you have to do—grammar. The *ni-* part of *nilikha* "created" is another one of those persnickety markers that something is real rather than made up. Then Tagalog has articles of a sort: the difference between the *ang*'s and *ng*'s is rather similar to that between *the* and *a*.

Yet a language can "care" about much less than these do. In Mandarin Chinese, *In the beginning, God created the heavens and the earth* is *Qǐ chū shén chuàng zào tiān dì*. Those words mean simply "start start God achieve make sky earth."

There are no endings of any kind. There is no marking of the past, no definite articles, and no plural marking. There is no marking of anything as an object, much less marking the "beginning" as located "at" a place. The Chinese speaker neither reminds their interlocutor that what they are saying is "actual" nor even has to link the words for the sky and the earth with a word for *and*! *Start start God achieve make sky earth.*

This is Chinese. For a Westerner, much of mastering the language is a matter of getting used to how very much does *not* have to be said. Yet it leads to a question. If languages that are bubbling over with fine-grained distinctions about materials and the definiteness or actuality of things are windows into the minds of their speakers, then what are we to suppose Chinese's grammar tells us about the minds of *its* speakers?

More generally, if it is true that what's in a language's grammar reveals to us what its speakers think about most readily, then what does a language suggest about its speakers when its grammar requires attention to relatively little? If Atsugewi represents a worldview, then it would seem that the worldview of the Chinese is rather uncomprehending and barren.

Whorf, in a less-often quoted passage, seems to have anticipated that his framework required some kind of address of the variable complexity among languages, venturing that "it may turn out that the simpler a language becomes overtly, the more it becomes dependent upon cryptotypes and other covert formations, the more it conceals unconscious presuppositions, and the more its lexations become variable and indefinable."

One senses that Whorf thought of these "covert formations," "unconscious presuppositions," and endlessly "indefinable" meanings as potentially weighty stuff. However, it is hard to imagine what scientific approach could illuminate such obscurity and murkiness. The whole idea is close to saying that English speakers have thoughts while Chinese speakers merely have notions.

Whorfianism, here, seems dangerous.

A Blooming Mess

And that has hardly been a renegade sentiment where Chinese is concerned. After all, the nature of Chinese grammar is such that one might venture that speaking Chinese makes one see the world not just differently, but dimly. There has been academic speculation along exactly those lines, and predictably, the wonder and romance that traditionally greets Whorfianism fell instantly away. The question is what this means for the whole enterprise.

The case in question is that of psychologist Alfred Bloom, in the early eighties. Bloom did nothing but follow in the footsteps of what was even by then decades of Whorfian work, and investigated whether how Chinese works affects how Chinese people think. However, this time, his focus was not on multiple words for colors or bouquets of words indexing what things are made of, but an absence of something.

Namely, a language like English is highly particular in encoding hypotheticality. To an English speaker, it seems as normal as the law of gravity that there are three similar but different sentences such as:

If you see my sister, you'll know she is pregnant.
If you saw my sister, you'd know she was pregnant.
If you had seen my sister, you'd have known she was pregnant.

The three connote different shades of nonreality; the first (*If you see my sister...*) implies that something will likely happen. The second (*If you saw my sister...*) makes the business an imagined scenario. The third (*If you had seen my sister...*) shifts the entire matter, complete with its hypotheticality, into the past.

In Mandarin Chinese, only with a studious elaboration unnecessary to casual speech could one convey those differences. All three sentences would be rendered as "If you see my sister, you know she is pregnant," without the specific marking of pastness and the conditional (*you'd*, i.e., *you would*) that English uses as a matter of course.

Here, then, is another example of how in Chinese, in the relative sense, one simply doesn't have to say much. Word for word the rendition is roughly "If you see I sister you know she pregnant get" for *all three* of the English sentences. So: if separate words for dark blue and light blue mean Russians perceive shades of blue "more" or "faster" than we do, and if an array of words marking what things are made of means that the Japanese process material "more" or "faster" than we do, then certainly if Chinese marks the hypothetical less explicitly than English, then the Chinese process hypotheticality "less" or "more slowly" than...

You can likely imagine the response.

It wasn't a witch hunt, but it elicited a suspiciously long trail of reply articles compared to cozier Whorfian work, especially for a book published long before the Internet era. There have been five major anti-Bloom pieces, trucking all the way up to 2005, a quarter century after Bloom's book appeared, by which time he had long ago moved on intellectually and occupationally. One also gleans, in the reception, a certain visceral component between the lines. All of the responses are thoroughly professional and civil, but the title of one is "A Response to Alfred Bloom"—why so personal? More typical would be "A Response to Bloom (1981)" or no mention of his name at all. Or, the subtitle of another one is "Picking Up the Pieces"— what broke? There would seem to have been what some processed as a bit of a brawl.

Frankly, there would almost certainly have been one if Bloom published his work in our era. Talk about your hypothetical—*if* Bloom ventured that Chinese makes its speakers less attuned to the difference between the real and the imagined today, then today he *would* be roasted in the blogosphere for months. It's not an accident that Peter Gordon's and Dan Everett's claims about the Pirahã have elicited an analogous volume of academic resistance, as Whorfian work highlighting deficit rather than advantage.

Yet Bloom did not just toss out his speculation without demonstration. He presented Chinese and American subjects with a story that could be interpreted counterfactually or concretely. Seven percent of the Chinese speakers chose the counterfactual interpretation, while 98 percent of the Americans did. He also posed to Chinese speakers perfectly plausible questions such as "If all circles were large and this small triangle were a circle, would it be large?" He found that far too often for it to be accidental, his subjects answered along the lines of "No! How can a circle be a triangle? How can this small circle be large? What do you mean?" English speakers had this response much, much less often.

Bloom, in exactly the same tradition of thought that people have found so attractive when applied to heightened sensibilities among Native Americans, concluded that speaking a language leaving much hypotheticality to context leaves a person's thought patterns less attuned to it than an English speaker's.

Over the years, researchers responding to Bloom have gotten different results from his. Their interpretations as to why involve how degrees of experience with English affect Chinese people's responses to such questions, how felicitous Bloom's translations into Chinese were, and Chinese people's possibly being better at grappling with hypotheticality applied to ordinary situations rather than deliberately abstract ones. Yet, Bloom of course offered responses to the responses.

At the end of the day, the observer's verdict is that Bloom was on to something, but not in a way that Whorf would have found especially compelling. There were hints of the truth even in the responses Bloom got at the outset, when subjects tended to object to the peculiar "what if" questions as "unnatural," "un-Chinese," "confusing," and "Western." Bloom's approach was to guess that these responses were surface manifestations of something driven ultimately by language affecting thought. However, just as plausible is that these thoughts represented, well, thought.

More specifically, could it not be that there is something in *being* Chinese, not speaking Chinese, that occasions a less ready engagement with useless brain-teaser questions like the ones about triangles being, just for the sake of argument, circles?

Evidence for that argument would be if speakers of a language as rich in markers of hypotheticality as English were as uncomfortable pretending triangles are circles as the Chinese subjects were. That evidence exists.

Linguist Donna Lardiere has shown that Arabic speakers sound quite "Chinese" when presented with what are, ultimately, silly questions. Arabic is not a telegraphic language in the slightest. It has explicit grammatical machinery to, if necessary, situate hypotheticality in the past to yield pluperfect *if I had* and conditional *would*-style meanings if necessary, such that "If you see I sister you know she pregnant get" seems just as queerly elementary to an Arabic speaker as it does to an English speaker. Yet Lardiere found that when presented with questions like the triangle bit, Arabs typically had responses such as: When you learn something you learn as it is—a circle is a circle, get what I mean? And a triangle could never be a circle. . . . If I agreed with this, it means I'm disagreeing with everything I did in math, it's like, how could an orange be an apple? Well, I don't think it's possible.

It would seem that we are dealing indeed with a difference in mindsets, but conditioned by culture rather than language. The main lesson is actually that the very familiarity a reader of this book is likely to have with counterfactual questions like the one about circles and triangles is a cultural trait rather than a human universal. As Lardiere notes, it is hardly just Chinese and Arab people who are often thrown by direct questions unconnected to utilitarian context. Studies such as linguistic anthropologist Shirley Brice Heath's classic *Ways with Words* demonstrate that direct and out-of-context questions themselves, along the lines of "What is the capital of South Dakota?," are an artifice of educational procedure much less natural in oral cultures in general, in which the direct question is often processed even as abrupt and confrontational. This possibly explains differentials in educational success between middle-class and less fortunate children (of all races) in the United States.

Equally pertinent is fascinating work in the 1930s by A. R. Luria in what is now Uzbekistan and Kyrgyzstan with illiterate or near-illiterate peasants. For example, Luria asked subjects "in the far north, where there is snow, all bears are white. Novaya Zembla is in the far north and there is always snow there. What color are the bears?" Responses ranged along the lines of "I don't know. I've seen a black bear. I've never seen any others…each locality has its own animals." Sound familiar? Respondents tended to find the very idea of answering questions disconnected from real-world utility idle, boring, and even faintly ridiculous.

There are endless directions to go in from the fact that human cultures and subcultures differ in their openness to engagement with questions that are abstract for their own sake. However, the evidence for this mindset being created by an absence of particular words or constructions that translate as, say, *I would have been* or *I had been* has not held up. And on Chinese in particular, we might question whether we would have wanted it to, because it would signal something much larger.

Namely, if no way to indicate *I would have been* or *I had been* in your language leaves you slow to wrap your head around the hypothetical, then imagine what we would be faced with in Chinese's lack of so very much else. Chinese has no definite articles. It has no marking of past and future—no *I walked* or *I will walk*; tense is often just left to context and they do just fine. It has no difference between *he*, *she*, and *it*, or evidential markers, and forget about any subjunctive. It does not even usually mark things as plural. Chinese, overall, takes it light. Really light.

And let's imagine: one careful article after another about all of these grammatical nonfeatures could possibly make a case about Chinese "shaping thought" in rendering its speakers infinitesimally less sensitive to such nuances of living. And the result would be a loomingly miserable proposition, which, no matter how artfully phrased, would constitute a grisly case that to be Chinese is to be not especially quick on the uptake.

Condemnation would be swift and indignant, and it is here that it becomes urgent to reconsider that the psychological differences revealed in even the finer Whorfian experiments are so small. When the results can potentially be framed as meaning that some people perceive time as vertical, or process differentials of blueness as "popping" enough to contort their take on paintings from Picasso's blue period, many will seek ways of reading those small differences as having some kind of larger import. However, as it happens, the controversy over Bloom's work actually leaves hints of the same kind of small but present result, suggesting some shade of influence from language upon thought.

Bloom, in one wing of his project, found that Chinese-English bilinguals performed better than Chinese monolinguals, concluding that commanding English affords a person a connection with hypotheticality that someone speaking only Chinese lacks. Also, L. G. Liu and then David Yeh and Dedre Gentner have shown that Chinese speakers perceive counterfactuality more readily when presented with familiar situations rather than abstract ones—upon which the fact remains that English speakers display that differential much less. That is, there may be something about English and hearkening to the difference between the real and the possible.

Here, however, where we are faced with the Chinese possibly exhibiting a handicap, note how much less savory it seems to magnify squeaky differentials laboriously glimpsed under artificial conditions into a statement about a people and how they wield their cognition amid this thing called life.

Choosing Which Differences Matter

Plural marking in Chinese as compared to other languages helps illuminate the heart of the issue.

Chinese doesn't care much about how many things there are. Things are marked for plural only for explicitness and more when they are alive; otherwise, for the most part plurality is left to context and no one bats an eye. It's European languages, among others, that are oddly strict about indicating overtly whenever there is more than one of something. Notice that the previous sentence would have been thoroughly processible if one could say, "It's European *language* that is oddly strict...."

Take Genesis again: English has "And God said, 'Let the waters bring forth swarms of living creatures, and let birds fly above the earth.'" Chinese has "God say water force much much multiply have life life of matter, and have sparrow bird fly at ground above" (*Shén shuō shuǐ yāo duō duō zī shēng yǒu shēng mìng de wù, yāo yǒu qiǎo què niǎo fēi zài dì miān yǐ shàng*). Chinese shows us that plural marking, seemingly so normal, is actually, as languages go, a tic, an obsessive-compulsive disorder that a language might wend its way into. Atsugewi means you just have to specify what kind of moving, and into what, and don't forget to always show that a noun is what it is, a noun. In the same way, English is a contract under which you agree to always specify overtly that there was more than one of something. Something bubbles up somewhere in any language.

Yet it is hardly inconceivable that a Whorfian experiment could be devised that showed that Chinese speakers, in some way, to some extent, are—quite slightly—less vividly attuned to how many of something there is when presented with, say, two rather than one objects on a screen. Why not, after all? In the introduction I noted that Whorfianism has been problematic in tending to only examine a few languages at a time, but Whorfianism has also only examined a highly constrained set of grammatical features. If language shapes thought, then what decides which aspects of it do so? Why not how a language encodes the plural?

Or doesn't? On Chinese's wan commitment to marking plurality, a Whorfian take would presumably have to be that as elsewhere, "language shapes thought." Yet most of us would wonder whether we were really to process Chinese people as significantly less attuned to there being two cups that need washing rather than just one, that two buses went by instead of one, and that there are two people in the living room rather than just one. Or: if Chinese people do process twoness a nano-peep less alertly than English speakers, is it to an extent that anyone could reasonably consider a different way of processing existence?

We gain perspective on the notion in viewing it from the other extreme. Suppose a language could be analyzed as making its speakers even *more* attuned to plurality than English? Suppose a language were one of the ones, say, of a breed in Africa Westerners are rarely aware of, such as the one spoken by the tragically burdened people of Darfur?

In their language, called Fur (Darfur means "the land of the Fur"), plurality is basically irregular, period. In English you mark the plural with -*s* except for a dozen or so strange cases like *children*, *mice*, *geese*, and *men*. But imagine a language where almost all plurals were like that! That's Fur. Thief: *kaam*. Thieves: *kaama*. But eye: *nuunga*, eyes—*kuungi*. You think child/children is odd? Try Fur: child, *kwe*. Children, though, is *dogala*! And that's how it is for all nouns—you just have to know.

In a language related to Fur, Sudan's Dinka, fire is *biñ* while fires is *biiiñ* where you make the *i* in the middle three times as long (yes, you really do!). Palm fruit is *tuuk* said on a low tone; say it on a high tone and you get palm *fruits*. Man: *mooc*. Men: *Rooor*! Women roar too—woman: *tiik*; women: *djaaar*! But hippos don't: one of them is a *roow*, two of them are *root*, and you just have to know, just like you have to know that one blade of grass is a *nooon* while if there are more, they have one less *o* and are *noon*, and on and on, with every noun.

There is barely anywhere to grab on. And it could be taken as meat for a Whorfian analysis. Remember: if Russian has separate words for dark blue and light blue, then that means Russians perceive shades of blueness meaningfully more vividly than English speakers. Okay: but it follows that we might ask a like question. If Fur and Dinka speakers have randomly different words for two of something rather than one of something, then presumably that means that Fur and Dinka speakers perceive shades of plurality more vividly than English speakers. If the Russians have their blues, then the Fur have their eyes—*nuunga* and *kuungi*—different "eyes" on the world, right?

And just suppose an experiment showed speakers of these languages hitting a button just a whisper faster than someone from New Haven when they saw a picture on a screen switch from depicting one house to depicting two. Or, presented with a big square with two dots in it, hitting the button faster when the screen added underneath a picture of two cows rather than one.

I lack the cleverness of the top-class Neo-Whorfians; they could devise an apter experiment. But I seek a larger point. Many are receptive to the idea of Russians with their blues, or Europeans and their tables talking with high voices—that's from a study that showed that speakers of languages that assign gender to inanimate objects are statistically more likely to imagine them with traits corresponding to the "sex" they belong to. But fewer would cotton to the idea that in real life, in a fashion that the humanist or an interested NPR-listening layman ought heed, certain African tribespeople process the difference between one dog and two more immediately than those reading this book.

One assumes that whatever a psychological experiment might eke out of a person in an artificial context, whatever eensy-weensy differences on that score one might find in the cosseted context of a psychological experiment, all human beings are in the same mental boat on one versus two, in terms of what could impact anything we know as this life we are all living, how we deal with it, and what we create on its basis.

What's cool about Dinka is that all the plurals are irregular. All languages are, in their own ways, as utterly awesome as creatures, snowflakes, Haydn string quartets, or what *The Magnificent Ambersons* would have been like if Orson Welles had been allowed to do the final edit. What's cool about Dinka is not, however, that it makes its speakers quirkily alert to there being more than one of something.

* * *

The question is why that same verdict doesn't apply to the Russian blues, the Japanese and their materials, or even that other trait Whorfianism has applied to the Chinese, their supposedly vertical sense of time. The Whorfian objects: "Of course all people process plural versus singular—but we're on to things like vision and sensation and time." Yet I am aware of no analysis spelling out just why vision and time are more pertinent to cognition than something as basic to experience as number. No matter what clever studies showed about differentials within milliseconds of response, no researcher would gain any traction from claiming that a goatherder in central Africa is more alive than an accountant in Minneapolis or a shoemaker outside of Beijing to there being two people in front of him than one. Why, then, would differentials in milliseconds about anything else in a language shed significant light on something as portentous as How People See the World?

Whatever the responses might be, they would have to square with the fact that there are countless languages in the world that present the speaker of a European language not with *more*—dark blue and light blue—but *less*. Some of them don't even have a word for *less*. In the rain forest of Surinam in South America, descendants of slaves who escaped plantations in the country in the 1600s live today in thriving communities, speaking their own language called Saramaccan. It's a blend of words and grammar from English, Portuguese, Dutch, and two African languages, and is not a variety of any of them, but very much a language of its own.

As a real language, it has its quirks. One of them is that to say *She is less naughty than him*, you must say *He is more naughty than her*; there simply is no word corresponding to *less*. There are many languages that have no word for *less* of this kind; if you think about it, it doesn't matter—as long as there is a way to say *more*, *less* is, technically, a frill. You can always express a thought via mentioning the element that is more rather than the one that is, consequently, less.

Does this mean that Saramaccans, living life as vividly as we do, are less attuned to differences in degree than other people?

And more to the point, note how unlikely it is that anyone would attempt to find out, despite Whorfianism's supposed purely intellectual interest in whether language shapes thought. In comparing other languages with English, the Whorfian quest is fonder of the mores than of the lesses, as it were.

This, however, makes hundreds of languages of East and Southeast Asia risky business for Whorfianism, as they pattern much like Chinese. If the Laotian in his language says *Aren't you afraid the boss will be disgusted when you are preparing food?*, he expresses it as "You not fear boss crap-disgust right?, you make eat?" No tense, no articles, no *-ing*, no *when* conjunction. If language affects thought, then what kind of thought are we to attribute to the population of Laos? Or Thailand, given that Thai and Laotian are essentially the same language?

Here, there is a possible objection. Of course, there are things in a language for a Whorfian to investigate beyond how much or little it marks overtly. We have even seen this with Chinese, in studies of whether its speakers process time vertically: this refers not to how detailed Chinese's marking of time is or is not, but simply in what kind of words it happens to use for the purpose. However, this leaves my question in this chapter standing and just as urgent.

Here's why. All languages differ from other ones in countless random ways analogous to English's *next month* being *the month below* in Chinese. For instance, just for this expression it's *the month that comes* in Spanish, *the following month* in Russian, *front month* in Indonesian, and so forth. Yet besides this kind of six-of-one / a-half-dozen-of-the-other differentiation between all languages, Chinese remains distinct from so very many of them in a particular way: its laconic essence compared to European and most other languages.

That quality stands eternally alongside the *month below* kind of things, and as Alfred Bloom saw, would seem to be as subject to Whorfian questions about how language shapes thought as anything else. Yet, for example, the Bloom study is not even mentioned in Deutscher's *Through the Language Glass*. As honest as that book is about how Whorfianism has fared, perhaps the Bloom story seems too utterly awkward to allow any room for languages as different pairs of glasses.

The take-home message is that language varies awesomely *despite* a single basic human cognition. The take-home message is not, however, that how languages vary teaches us about how cognitions vary. Tempting as the latter analysis may be, it will eternally run up against things such as that across Indonesia, the way to render *Someone is eating the chicken* in casual speech can be just *Chicken eat!* Anyone who has spent time in Indonesia will readily attest that the nation's people are vastly more reflective than anything a sentence like that—typical of much colloquial Indonesian—suggests about language shaping their thoughts. Where is the warmly received Whorfian literature about how certain languages might make their speakers *less* aware of something central to existence? My goal in this book is to show that the essence of language absolves us from having to even treat that as a problem.

And a problem it is. Take the possible riposte that I am caricaturing Whorfian work, when it only *suggests* that a language makes its speakers only *somewhat* more likely to think in certain ways. Just somewhat. That riposte is well and good when applied to how vividly someone might perceive gradations of blue, or even how vertically someone might perceive time going by. But that riposte also boxes one into agreeing that the telegraphic nature of Chinese *suggests* that its speakers are *somewhat* dumb. Let's not caricature—just somewhat. But still. If you want the grits you have to take the gravy.

To wit, if when faced with Chinese's telegraphic quality the proper response is to suppose that any cognitive consequences are too minimal to be treated as affecting thought and culture, then one must ask why the verdict is not the same even when the data happen to suggest greater, rather than lesser, alertness to some aspect of being human.

Whorfianism and Thrift

Might there be a way to mine Whorfian gold from the terseness of Chinese nevertheless? It's been tried, in a pleasantly oddball fashion. I always suspected someone would try it, as there is a precedent for its approach in a passing idea some linguists venture on a related topic.

A truism in the academic linguistics realm is that all languages are equally complex. The truism is well intentioned and even benevolent, in that it stems from a quest to demonstrate that languages of "undeveloped" groups are not jibberish. Linguist / anthropologists of the early twentieth century of the kind who influenced Whorf, such as Edward Sapir and Franz Boas, set this discovery in stone, showing that Native

American languages like Navajo are, if anything, more complex than French and German.

They are—boy, are they! However, the fundamentally advocational and defensive stance here—itself invaluable—settled into a general recoil from the idea that any language could be less complex than any other one. That sense reigns still among linguists, anthropologists, and fellow travelers. Yet it is impossible not to notice that when it comes to complexity, languages do differ.

No one who knows English and Chinese could miss what we have seen in this chapter, that overall, you simply have to say less in a typical Chinese sentence than in an English one. However, what's less known to most is that compared to possibly most of the world's languages, English is rather like Chinese. For example, in languages like the one used on Rossel Island off of Papua New Guinea that I mention in chapter 2, in the typical sentence you have to pack in things an English speaker would never dream of having to actually attend to, such as endlessly fine shades of what it is to be *on* something, or even using assorted suffixes to indicate whether the *he* or *she* you mention is the person you were just talking about or some new *he* or *she*, or even other suffixes to show whether you are *doing* something (like walking) or just *undergoing* something (like falling). Some languages are just much busier than others.

In response to this, knowing that some languages also attend to much less of the nuance of reality than that—for example, Chinese—some linguists fashion a way of maintaining the idea that all languages are equally complex: the idea that having to glean something from context is, in itself, a kind of complexity. Under this analysis, there are two kinds of complexity. It's complexity that English has to mark something as happening in the past with *-ed* or to carefully index grades of hypotheticality with the *if*'s and *then*'s and conditional mood and such. But then it's also complexity that in Chinese you have to glean those kinds of things from context. That is, reliance on context is, itself, complex.

Well, okay. I find the idea forced, and no one has ever demonstrated it scientifically. However, it's always out there, and it means that it's only a matter of time before someone proposes that in Chinese, since absence is complexity too, *not* having a grammatical trait can force attention to something just as *having* it can.

That is exactly what Yale economist Keith Chen has put forward about Chinese and other languages. His thesis is peculiar and bold. Chinese does not have a future tense marker along the lines of English's *will*. Many languages don't and leave future largely to context. Chen proposes that in countries with languages that don't mark the future regularly, like China, the absence of the future marking makes people pay *more* attention to futurity—and makes them more likely to save money! And pay more attention to preventative health practices and such. To be clear: the idea isn't that *having* a future marker makes you pay more attention to the future, rather, *not* having one does.

Needless to say, the media loved this, especially with Chen providing the deeply quantified kind of analysis economists are trained in. Might it be that quietly, how people's grammars

work has actually had an impact on their countries' econo-
mies? As weird as that seems, might it be that the truth, however bizarre the notion seems, is in the numbers?

No, I'm afraid not. A swell graph of Chen's allows us to find
the actual truth. The dark bars are languages that mark the
future pretty religiously, in the way that an English speaker
thinks of as normal: for example, *I walk, I walked, I will walk.*
The light bars are the languages where the future is largely left
to context—which worldwide, is actually quite common.

Chen presents the graph as showing that future-marking
languages cluster among the countries with *lower* savings rates.
Already, we see that despite the statistical fact that countries
with future-marking languages save 4.75 percent less, the
overall picture leans discomfitingly toward a rather scattered
distribution of dark and light bars—some light ones amid the
dark, and lots of dark ones amid the light. The statistics show
the reality? Sure—but only if the linguistic analysis is solid.
And it happens not to be.

Chen, although making a diligent effort to consult the
grammars, was misled by the fact that ultimately, grammars
can be unreliable when it comes to explaining whether or not
a language "marks the future" as regularly as English does. For
example, Chen has Russian as a future-marking language. And
indeed, you can get that impression from a grammar of Russian that devotes itself to telling an English speaker that you
express the future by doing *x*, *y*, and *z*. However, Russian does
not have anything you could call a future marker in the sense
of English *will* or the future tense conjugations you might
recall in French and Spanish.

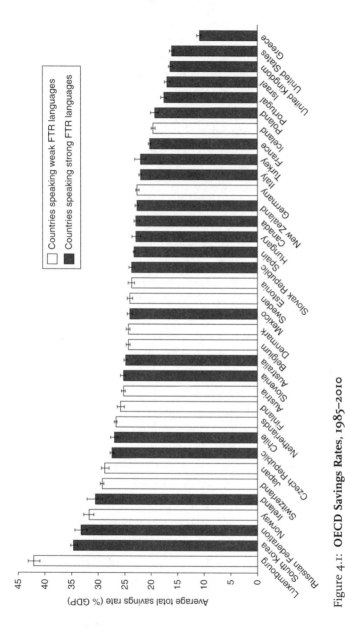

Figure 4.1: **OECD Savings Rates, 1985–2010**

Note: On average, countries that speak strong FTR languages save 4.75% less. t = 2.77, p = 0.009

It is part of learning Russian, in fact, to wrap your head around expressing the future by implying it, through bits of stuff that mean other things. It wasn't for nothing that literary critic Edmund Wilson once ventured—possibly having drunk in some Whorfianism—that Russians' inability to be on time was because Russian doesn't have a future tense.

Even English is like this to an extent: one says *We're buying the Honda Civic*, where we express something we will do in the future with the construction called the present progressive. Imagine someone asking, "So, what's going on about the car you want to buy?" If you respond, "We will buy the Honda Civic," you likely learned English last night.

In Russian, the future usually piggybacks this way on something else. The details are oppressive and, here, unnecessary, but suffice it to say that while in English the big distinction is between now, then, and later, in Russian the big distinction is between "flowing along" and "bang, right then," whether in the past, present, or future. The future, in Russian, is largely expressed as one of various takes on "bang, right then." So, *ja pisal* means "I **was writing**," that is, flowing along writing. But add *na-* and say *ja na-pisal* and it means "I wrote"—right then. Tell someone to write something (right now) and you say *Na-pishi!* In the same way, to say "I will write" you use that same *na-* bit and say *Na-pishu*. The idea is that you are not talking about just writing along, over a period of time— rather, you mean you will start some writing. Right now, writing will start.

But this means that in Russian, there is no marker you can think of as being specifically for expressing the future.

Russian offers no table of future tense endings to learn. A Russian struggles to explain to an English speaker what "the future in Russian" is, typically resorting to just giving examples like *na-pishu* whose endings, in terms of conjugation, are in the present tense. True, you can use the *be* verb to say "I'll **be** writing"—*ja budu pisat'*. This is the kind of thing Chen likely came across. But that's a highly secondary, also-ran kind of future—go back to the Honda conversation and imagine some poor soul saying, "I will be buying the Honda Civic." Only now and then do you need to say such things. Overall, to learn Russian as an English speaker is to ask, at some point, "How, exactly, do you put a verb in the future?"

So that means that on Chen's chart, the Russian bar should be white. Now, as it happens, if it were white, that would be good for Chen, because Russians are actually good savers. For him, Russian as a future-marking language is something he has to classify as "noise," because his idea is that languages that mark the future make their speakers save *less* money. But this actually creates more, not fewer problems.

Russian is part of a family of languages, the Slavic brood, that largely all work the same way. The facts on the future are the same for Czech, Slovak, and Polish. Predictably from his take on Russian, Chen codes all of them as future marking. Yet on his chart, Czechs are good savers (another problem even under his analysis), while Poles are bad ones, and Slovaks are somewhere in between.

This leaves Chen in a muddle no matter how we parse the data. We might say that even if Russian and friends don't have a word or prefix like *will* that is *only* for future, they do require a speaker to do *something* to make the future, even if that something can also be used for other things. So, we could say that calling them nonfuture languages is splitting hairs. But then, why are Russian, Czech, Slovak, and Polish spread all the way across the grid? Shouldn't they, if grammar shapes thrift, cluster?

But then if we accept that these four languages are *not* future marking and should all be white, then that distribution is still a fatal flaw. What is Polish, in particular, doing way over on the right with the bad savers, when Poles (as I have confirmed in exchanges with a Polish speaker while writing this) have the same hard time telling an English speaker how to "make a verb future" as Russians, and for the same reason? We might add that Czech and Slovak are essentially the same language—why would their speakers be so many bars apart if we are really seeing a meaningful correlation between grammar and having the discipline to save?

Meanwhile, Slovenian is also a Slavic language and, as it happens, it does have an actual future-marking construction. But on Chen's chart, aren't Slovenians a little too far leftward in the thrifty realm for people with a future-marker that supposedly should be discouraging them from socking funds away for a rainy day?

And there's some more. For example, Korean, too, requires an English speaker to give up the idea of a "future marker." Nothing in Korean corresponds to *will*—Chen may have gotten an impression otherwise from a suffix that is translatable as roughly "could" or "might." But that's not *will*.

Whether we keep the four Slavic bars black or white, their spreading all the way across the thriftiness grid, in combination with the Korean problem, renders Chen's chart a randomness. Ultimately, it comes down to this. Given how Chen's chart actually corresponds with the grammars in question—such as that future-marking Slovenian is right next to Anglophone Australia but *twenty-one bars leftward of* the Anglophone United States—how plausible is it that the reason savings rates in the United States have been so low has anything at all to do with the word *will?*

The Dog That Doesn't Bark

When a Study Shows a Negative

And so it goes. Even attempts to show links between what Chinese *does* have and how Chinese people think run aground. We have already seen how fragile the results are from investigating whether Mandarin's *month below* means that Mandarin speakers sense time as vertical in any significant way. In addition, an analogous problem has cropped up regarding something else present, rather than absent, in Mandarin. This time it's the same kind of markers of material that we saw in Japanese with the Nivea experiment.

In Japanese, when there's a number, recall, you have to stick in a little word that differs depending on what something is like. Two *hiki* of dogs, but two *hon* of beers, and so on. Chinese has the same "bubble": two *zhī* of dogs, two *tiáo* of rivers, and many more. To an extent, these little words correspond to actual qualities of the thing in question—for many animals, for many skinny things. However, they spill beyond that, to the extent that overall, speaking the language means just knowing which little word to use with which word, just "because." For example, why in Mandarin is it both two *bǎ* of scissors and two *bǎ* of umbrellas? You just have to live with it.

Yet Whorfianism entails that Mandarin speakers must think of scissors and umbrellas as alike on a certain level regardless, because—drum roll, please—language shapes thought. And then in other languages with little words like this that you have to use after numbers, they apply in alternately random ways. Remember how Japanese's *hon*, used with beer, is also used with things as unlike as pencils, phone calls, and movies? Whorfianism, then, also leads one to expect that speakers of other languages with such little words must mentally group things that happen to take the same one of them, such as Japanese—or Thai, where you say both two *tua* of eels and two *tua* of tables.

But in fact, speakers of such languages do not group objects that way. A study has shown that Mandarin speakers are as likely to feel scissors and eels alike as scissors and umbrellas, despite that in Mandarin, while scissors and umbrellas both require *bǎ*, eels, as skinny things, require *tiáo*. Meanwhile Thais are as likely to group eels and umbrellas as eels and tables, despite that in their language both eels and tables take *tua* while umbrellas take a different marker *kʰan*.

This study shows, quite simply, that despite Mandarin and Thai speakers using little words each indexed to often random assemblages of nouns day in and day out, they do not end up processing those objects as akin on any deep level. To wit, to speak Mandarin is not to be a human being who sees scissors and umbrellas as somehow alike in a way that any other rational human being would.

And in the end we must ask whether that is a surprise. It is no more one than that it doesn't add up that Mandarin speakers go around less aware of the difference between what is and what could be than English speakers. Languages differ. Thought doesn't. Or, if it does, it's because of cultural factors that are conditioned by—wait for it!—culture. Not grammar.

* * *

The Whorfian impulse will resist. Surely the data are not yet all in. But what are data? The relevant data here are "Start start God achieve make sky earth" and "If you see I sister you know she pregnant get." Billions—literally billions, if we count the speakers of Mandarin, the other Chinese varieties, and the innumerable similar languages spoken in East and Southeast Asia—of human beings speak in exactly that way day in and day out, and have since time immemorial.

Cherish Whorfianism as showing that all people are cognitively advanced, or even cognitively interesting. But then admit that an imposing clutch of languages tend to relegate the obvious to the blankness of implication. And then try again to embrace the idea that language shapes thought. Studies show that it does—or better, that it *can*. Somewhat.

But is that "somewhat" robust enough that in light of what her grammar is like, we could tell a Mandarin speaker she's a bit of a dummy?

CHAPTER 5

What's the Worldview from English?

WHORFIAN WORK COMPARES ENGLISH with other languages, with the goal of showing how other languages might make other people think differently from English speakers. However, something investigated too infrequently, which could be useful in evaluating the implications often drawn from Whorfian work, is how English might make us think differently from other people.

It could be said that this is what the work on other languages has shown, although not presented in quite that way. If Russians perceive dark blue and light blue as more distinct than we do, then we perceive them as rather less distinct than they do. If some native Australians process themselves as oriented toward geographical coordinates, then what defines us is that we do not.

However, facts such as these feel somewhat beside the point. So often it seems to be English speakers who don't rather than do, who are somewhat less sensitive to something, who lack what others have. Surely there isn't something inherently numbing about our language, however: any appearance of that would have to be an artifact of experiments typically done by English speakers for an Anglophone audience.

The question, then, is: How does English shapes its speakers' thought, in ways that would intrigue audiences if most Whorfian work were done from the perspective of Third World languages, or even Japanese or Chinese? Of course there is no need to suppose that English outright bars us from thinking anything, any more than any language exerts such an effect on its speakers. We established early in the book that modern Whorfianism is about statistical tendencies, not straw-man absolutes. But still: How does English influence the thinking patterns of those who speak it?

Many will already notice how peculiar the question feels. The idea that our language creates a uniquely Anglophone "worldview" can seem less intuitive than that Japanese creates a Japanese worldview. It isn't hard to imagine a language called Guugu Yimithirr creating its own worldview, since its very name suggests a world of life vastly unlike our own. But when it comes to future tense markers, ways of saying *before* and *after*, or nonexistent gender markers on nouns, what worldview are they creating for the man reaching for a box of cereal at a Walmart outside of St. Louis?

The question bears exploration. In this chapter we will settle in with just a single sentence of English and train the Whorfian light upon it in the same fashion as we usually see it trained on other languages. However, we will not examine a passage from the Bible or Henry James or even Henry Miller: we want live, spoken language. And then, not from Walter Cronkite or Hillary Clinton either. We must keep front and center that in framing languages as shaping thought, we are referring not to icons speaking carefully to large audiences, but real people speaking casually amid everyday life.

As real and live, for example, as a guy of about sixteen I overheard saying something one weekday morning in Jersey City on his way to school with a friend. He was black, for the record, and that aspect of him is in itself handy, in that any claims about how English shapes thought must be applicable to him as well as to a middle-aged person who subscribes to the *Atlantic*—in treating English as shaping thought, we must account for a vast array of people, and for that matter, not only in the United States but worldwide. Besides, to the extent that this guy's rendition of the sentence was affected by the patterns of the dialect widely known as Ebonics, those, too, are richly pertinent to evaluating what to make of Whorfian findings on language and thought.

Recall: those findings certainly show that language can shape thought to an infinitesimal degree. The question is what implications we draw from that degree about what it is to be human. In that light, here is what a human said to his friend one morning in 2012: "Dey try to cook it too fast, I'm-a be eatin' some pink meat!"

If anyone needs translation, the standard version would be *If they try to cook it too fast, I'm going to be eating some pink meat!* I didn't catch what came before or afterward; I just kind of liked the feel of the sentence such that it stuck in my ear and later occurred to me as solidly, even pleasantly, representative modern American English.

So: we know that if we asked our teen to participate in certain kinds of psycholinguistic experiments, we would see that his modern American English shapes his thought in certain ways. However, how plausible would we find the assertion that his speech—*Dey try to cook it too fast, I'm-a be eatin' some pink meat!*—conditions in him a worldview (1) different from that of an Indonesian or a Brazilian and (2) akin to that of Lindsay Lohan, Condoleezza Rice, Ben Kingsley, me, and probably you?

We shall see.

As If

The first order of business, according to Whorfian tradition, is to subject our teen to the same gloomy surmise that has been tried on the Chinese to such general dismay. Namely, if language shapes thought, then mustn't we wonder what it might mean that the guy did not use the word *if*?

More precisely, sometimes he uses *if* and sometimes he doesn't: black Americans shift in and out of the structures of Black English. Still, though, it is presumably reasonable to hypothesize that someone with lower rates of *if* usage is having their thoughts shaped less by *if*-ness than someone whose dialect requires them to use *if* always.

As it happens, there is a long history of treating Black English exactly in this vein. Often it has been with good intentions based on a fallacy: that black children need rescue from an illogical home dialect. Education expert Carl Bereiter and his associates in the 1960s argued that a sentence like *They mine* for *They are mine* was, in its lack of a *be* form, a broken locution hindering the learning process. However, since mighty languages like Russian and Indonesian also do not use a *be* verb in the same way, Bereiter was unknowingly diagnosing massive numbers of human beings as verbally handicapped (for the record, the writers of the Old Testament would also have to be included, as Biblical Hebrew was *be*-less in the same way).

It should be said that Bereiter's analysis was rooted in a sincere desire to help poor black children learn to read more effectively. In fact, the method of teaching reading to poor kids that my friend Siegfried Englemann and Bereiter spearheaded, which itself does not dwell on issues of Black English grammar, is one of the most tragically underconsulted secrets in education today. However, it should also be said that someone else treating Black English's streamlined nature as evidence of deficit around the same time was psychologist Arthur Jensen, who famously suggested that black people are, on the average, less intelligent than others.

Ah, yes—now what were we saying about "language shapes thought" and our black teenager? Most will readily classify treating his casual relationship to the word *if* as having about as much cognitive import as Chinese people's soft-pedaling of explicit ways of expressing *would* and *would have*. Any remaining sympathy anyone has for treating Black English as a deficit must also be prepared to assert that languagewise, Chinese speakers are also playing with less than a full deck. Reject that, and the only logical conclusion is that languages (and dialects of languages) differ in how explicit they are overall—here Atsugewi, there Chinese—but that this difference is independent of thought in any significant way, certainly not justifying metaphors about "how we see the world."

When it comes to how someone speaks English, this isn't even all that hard to wrap our heads around. After all, writing obscures things absolutely central to expression: context and intonation. The boy's friend did not hear *Dey try to cook it too fast* as an independent declaration, because they were both aware of the situation they were talking about, in which there was presumably some question as to the quality of the food. Also, the vocal melody with which the boy expressed *Dey try to cook it too fast* made it clear that something else, a result of this potentially rapid cooking, was coming up immediately. That is, because of the melody, of a sort that any English speaker would use when uttering a dependent clause of this kind, even if the boy had for some reason said *Dey try to cook it too fast* and then lapsed into silence, his friend would have wondered what was coming next. *If dey cook it too fast, den what? Say somethin', dude!*

This sentence was, then, one passage in a thoroughly coherent exchange. If language shapes thought, and what that boy was speaking was language, then apparently Whorfianism is not to be applied to his usage of *if*. We move on.

Dey In, Dey Out

To many, the idea that different languages condition different ways of feeling life is the most interesting thing about languages. Often, however, even just bits of language are interesting in a great many ways, quite apart from fragile Whorfian speculations. The little word *they* is a good example.

It started as a patch of sorts, entering the language from elsewhere, as a solution to a problem. Basically, in Old English the words for *he* and *they* had become rather inconveniently similar. *He* was pronounced "hay" and the word for *they* was roughly "hyay." By early Middle English, both *he* and *they* were *he*.

Stranger things have happened. What's the other language you have learned besides English where the word for *you* is the same in the singular and the plural? It would have seemed barbaric to earlier English speakers who kept *thou* for one person and *you* for more as religiously separate as we keep *I* and *we* apart today. There was even, in Old English, a pronoun just for saying "you *two*" as opposed to you all: *git!* But today, we consider the one-size-fits-all *you* as perfectly normal.

Yet languages have a way of keeping things organized to a certain extent. English speakers have always champed at the bit somewhat on the *you* issue, for example. Forms such as *y'all*, *youse*, and Pittsburgh's *y'uns*, despite their backyard repute, are attempts to be more explicit and make English more "normal" in this regard. The almost suffocating influence of the standard language in education and the media keeps these novelties from ever becoming accepted speech, but things were quite different in the fourteenth century. Before widespread schooling or literacy, natural attempts to tidy a language up (or muss it up) could normalize much more easily.

As such, Scandinavian Vikings confronting the singular/plural *he* puzzle found it handy to bring their own Old Norse's third-person plural pronoun into the slot.

That's how we got *they*: a linguistic cross-fertilization. We all know languages borrow words for new things, like sushi. However, we're less likely to think as meat-and-potatoes a word like *they* started as a foreign intrusion. Thou never knowest!

★ ★ ★

Meanwhile, however, if we train that Whorfian lens on naturalized little *they*, we fall back into the issue that yielded so little in the last chapter: whether people differ in how richly they perceive plurality.

The experiment would have to take into account that *they*, as languages go, is about average in terms of explicitness in third-person pronouns. English gilds the lily in even having a pronoun especially marking more than one third person, as we have seen: some languages have the same word for *he*, *she*, *it*, and *they*. Meanwhile, Old English had even more fun than modern English. I simplified a bit before: Old English's *hie* was the masculine *they*, but there was a feminine *they* too, *heo*, pronounced roughly as a doughty older character on *Downton Abbey* would pronounce *hair*: "hay-uh." Thus English was like Arabic and Hebrew and other languages in keeping things tidy. Yes, tidy; if you're going to have a *he* and a *she*, then shouldn't there be a *they* and, as it were, a female "they-uh"?

But my, how much further languages can take this kind of hair-splitting. Among languages in the South Seas eastward of Australia, it is ordinary for a language to have separate words for they two, they three (or so), and they all. Elsewhere things are just plain different from anything we would imagine. In the Amazon's Jarawara, if the things in question are inanimate objects, there is no pronoun for them at all. That's right: the pronoun is, of all things, absence. You know, as a Jarawara speaker, that when no pronoun is used, then it is a "phantom" *they*, referring to things that are not living ones.

Consider, in the light of all of this, a conclusion along the lines of Mark Abley's on Native American languages of the Algonquian group, such as Cree, Ojibwa, and Pocahontas's Powhatan. Abley, a journalist, is deeply taken with the Whorfian perspective, and for all of the right reasons in the sociopolitical sense. But it means that to him, "to speak properly, in an Algonquian language, is to be aware of the identities and interrelationships of all the people you address." He bases this statement on the fact that in such languages, when you use *I* and *you* in the same sentence such as *I see you*, the *you* comes before the *I*, such that one might think that the "I" is less central in Algonquians' minds than in ours.

One might make a similar statement based on the proliferation of *they* words in languages like the ones I mentioned in the South Seas—especially since such languages are similarly fecund in their variations on *we* and *you*. Also, many might find the Abley approach welcome in comparing undersung, undervalued, and historically exploited groups of the Melanesian islands to speakers of boring, oppressive English. Under this analysis, to speak English would mean being relatively insensitive to people, their number, and their relationships to you and to one another, less socially fine-tuned than, say, a Melanesian.

However, besides the air of Noble Savage–style romanticization in this kind of thing, as well as how shaky the idea is that Anglophones worldwide are inherently a little chilly, does the Abley-style perspective on *they* seem as attractive when we compare the Melanesians not to Margaret Thatcher but to a black teenager in Jersey City? English is likely the only language he's ever known, and yet the language that supposedly shapes his thoughts is the same one shaping the thoughts of Rush Limbaugh.

At such a point many will consider that the entire enterprise just doesn't hold up. Adding fuel to that fire would be if we decide that in having a distinction between third-person singular and plural at all in his pronouns, our Jersey City boy is "aware of the identities and interrelationships of all the people you address" to a *greater* extent than the Pirahã tribespeople. They have a single *he/she/it/they* pronoun. Yet they live in a small group, interacting closely all day long every day. Wouldn't we expect them to be *more* attuned to shades of *they*-ness than an urban American? But if we would, then that's yet another mark against a meaningful connection between how a language's grammar plays out and how its speakers think.

And then who knows what kind of connection we could draw between grammar and reality based on the Jarawara's lack of any pronoun at all for inanimate objects! If asked, I'm sure they would tell us that they perceive that birds are alive and sticks aren't just as clearly as we do, thank you very much. I'm not sure who would tell them otherwise—or even venture an experiment seeking to reveal them as a hair less quick at pressing a button related to demonstrating that fact. And then, were Old English villagers more alert to the *gender* of *pairs* of people than a fifteen-year-old boy in Jersey City? Why?

And so it goes. Sometimes a cigar is just a cigar, and sometimes, a *they* is just a *they*. Onward!

Try, Try Again

Try is an orphan. No one knows where it came from beyond a certain point: roughly, somewhere around France. It's one of the thousands of words that English borrowed (and never gave back) from French in the Middle English period, leaving English's vocabulary the queer blend of grand old Germanic and fancy new French and Latin that it mainly is. The French word *trier* was one of assorted variants of that word kicking around in the French area and thereabouts. Just as one can know from comparing dogs, platypuses, kangaroos, and more that there was once an Ur-mammal with four legs and hair that gave birth to live young, comparing the variations on *trier* we can know that there was once a word *triare* in the Gallic area.

Usually, one can then compare a word like this to similar ones in other languages throughout Europe, and using the same comparative method, linguists have reconstructed thousands of words in what must have been the grandfather language to most of the languages of Europe, not to mention Iran and India. For example, *father* began as a word *pəter* in that ancient language, at this point pretty firmly placed as having been spoken in the southern Ukraine. It yielded French's *père*, Spanish's *padre*, German's *Vater*, Hindi's *pitaa*, Irish's *atheir*, Armenian's *hayr*, and so on.

But there's no word like *triare* in any other European languages. That means *try* has no pedigree tracing back to some ancestral word that now has its spawn in Russian, Greek, Hindi, Persian, and Lithuanian. And only because of France's temporary takeover of England in the late Middle Ages, when

French was the language of writing and its words percolated into humble English speech, did the word make it even into English.

Try, then, is a foster child, shipped across the English Channel around the time Thomas Aquinas was teaching at the University of Paris and today is used several times a day by English speakers worldwide, including on ordinary weekday mornings by adolescents in Jersey City, New Jersey.

★ ★ ★

And how our particular adolescent used *try* on one particular morning is especially interesting. Note he said *Dey try to cook it too fast, I'm-a be eatin' some pink meat!* If you think about it, that usage of *try* is somewhat off in the logical sense if we take *try* as intended in its core meaning. It would be one thing if he said, *If they try to cook it too fast, I'm going to tell them to turn down the heat* or *If they try to cook it too fast, I just won't have any chicken.* Overall, if he says, *If they try to cook it too fast*, we expect that he will follow this up with something about him either stopping them from doing so or turning away from what they cook.

Instead, though, his sentence has him eating the meat that the people "tried to" cook too fast—that is, they would appear to have not tried to, but succeeded in, cooking the meat too fast, which makes you wonder why the guy put it as "try to" when, after all, they quite simply *did*. One feels as if the sentence should have been simply *If they cook it too fast, I'll be eating pink meat*—the *try to* seems extra.

And it is, but not in a random way. This usage of *try to* is actually an example of how the dialect of English that most black Americans switch in and out of all day, so often thought of as "bad" grammar, a deformation of "correct" English, is in many ways more complex than standard English. Our adolescent's usage of *try to* is, of all things, a subjunctive mood a-borning in Black English.

Its air of extraness is analogous to how the subjunctive in languages like Spanish feels to English speakers. In Spanish, for *I doubt you will go* is *Dudo que él* **vaya**, where the subjunctive form *vaya* conveys the hypotheticality of the going instead of the plain-vanilla indicative *va*. To an English speaker learning Spanish this seems a finicky add-on. One wonders why a language has to actually have a separate verb form to mark such a nuance. In the same way, the *try to* in *Dey try to cook it too fast, I'm-a be eatin' some pink meat* is marking the hypothetical.

Indeed, taken literally the *try to* seems like clutter, "messy" grammar. However, black people use *try to* in precisely this way quite often. It is a regularity, a logical pattern of, of all things, grammar.

That is, *try to* has broken the bonds of the literal and now signifies *"In the case that* they cook it too fast." This kind of thing happens to words in all languages all the time, such as English, where *going to* now means future—*I'm going to think about that*—even though in terms of the original meaning of *go*, that doesn't make sense: how do you "go" toward thinking? *Going to* has only been used that way since the 1600s. To a speaker of Old English, using *going to* to express the future would sound as odd as our teen's use of *try to* does to many of us now.

"Us" would include the very people who are using it that way, if we were to tell them they were doing so. To be sure, black Americans are no more consciously aware that they are wielding a nascent subjunctive than standard English speakers know that when they say *That must be the Indian food* they are using what is termed the *evidential mood* by linguists. Sources such as the online Urban Dictionary note a black "expression" *tryna*. This, however, is not the subjunctive *try to* but a mere matter of colloquial pronunciation, namely of the ordinary *try-ing to*, used just as all English speakers use *try* in its default meaning. Our teen's *try to* usage is something different—and just as cool as the aural "flava" of *tryna* for *trying to*.

And this *try to* as in *try to cook it too fast* is a grammatical feature more elaborate than in schoolbook English, where the subjunctive has been on the ropes for centuries. One can slip it in. *If there be persons in opposition* is the subjunctive version of *If there are persons in opposition*, but it's decidedly hoity-toity. *If I were the one* versus *If I was the one*: the fact that grammar hounds must lecture us on how the *were* version, the subjunctive one, is better is a sign that it's dying. Yet our teen pops off with his *try to cook it too fast* intending nothing remotely formal, and certainly with no one having told him to express himself that way. He was just talking—using a subjunctive as effortlessly as someone speaking French or Spanish.

* * *

Those are some of the ways that *try to* is interesting. How does the Whorfian take on it stack up? Language shapes thought—and so now we have to speculate that black Americans are possibly more alert to the hypothetical than other Americans. It's one thing—although, as we have seen, a deeply fraught one—to speculate that Amazonian hunter-gatherers, with their evidential markers, might have an exotically different take on whether things are true and why than Westerners. But now, are we to say that the black cop in Oakland, or the black woman minister in Atlanta, or Kanye West, or Barack Obama, hearkens more keenly to the *if* over the *is* than Ashton Kutcher or Tom Friedman?

We should be wary of the whole approach after what came of Alfred Bloom's attempt to delineate Chinese people as *less* sensitive to the hypothetical. However, this time we are treating a people as *more* alive to what might be versus what is. Might that seem perhaps more inviting? Especially since it might serve to counter the tragically prevalent sense that black American speech is a perversion of English rather than a fascinating variation upon it? I might note that I myself have been very much on the battlefront when it comes to spreading the word on this latter point.

However, on the specific issue of black people and higher subjunctive awareness, we're asking for trouble in the scientific sense. For one, recall that this is the same dialect that can leave off the *if* in a sentence like *Dey try to cook it too fast, I'm-a be eatin' some pink meat*. That would seem to indicate leaving the hypothetical to context to a *greater* extent than standard English's obligatory use of the *if*. So which is it? If anything, the *try to* subjunctive combined with the absent *if* would seem to leave black Americans at par with, but not ahead of, standard English speakers on hypotheticality.

And then we run up against the bigger picture. Thought patterns drive culture. What, then, does the culture of black Americans have in common with that of Ancient Romans, whose Latin had a subjunctive, which then evolved into the subjunctive today used by speakers of the languages that developed from Latin, like French and Spanish? We might even ask what was the common thought pattern that meant that Ancient Romans, in addition to peasants in Gaul and Iberia, used a subjunctive—and, on top of that, not the Vietnamese, or any number of Australian Aboriginals, or Israelis or Finns, or countless other people one could easily parse as culturally likely to cotton to subjunctivity. To wit, Julius Caesar, Valéry Giscard d'Estaing, Pablo Picasso, Sophia Loren, and even Nicolae Ceauşescu have shared just *what* in common, that would indicate that the subjunctive in their language shaped their thoughts? And whatever that would be, now try to liken it to the way Jesse Jackson and Jay-Z process reality as well.

Here, it becomes attractive to consider those soup bubbles again, the ones that pop up on that side, this one, in the middle, God knows just where one will turn up—all you know is that some will, somewhere and always. There is an endless variety of life's nuances that a language may end up marking. All languages mark some but not all, and which ones they mark is a matter not of what its speakers need or what its speakers are like, but chance. Chance is what makes both Gérard Depardieu and our Jersey City black boy both use subjunctive marking, just as chance is why both the Tuyuca Amazonians and Bulgarians have evidential marking while Polynesian islanders and Czechs do not.

In fact, the way *try to* is used in Black English shows us that in the end, languages show that all people think alike, not differently. Black English can leave off an *if*—*Dey try to cook it too fast . . .* —but then, the *try to* subjunctive conveys the same kind of hypotheticality, just in a way less obvious. This is akin to what we saw in how Chinese, although lacking definite articles, can convey definiteness with word order, even though speakers do not consciously know it: *train arrived* means *the* train came, while *arrived train* means *a* train came.

Lesson: black Americans' dialect is more subjunctive grammatically than standard English. However, any attempt to extend that into characterizing speakers of that dialect as fascinatingly attuned to the *if* over the *is* fails, once we consider how likely we would be to parse Leslie Caron and Ségolène Royal, all of the peoples of Portugal, Spain, Latin America, France, Italy, and even Romania as subject to the same influence of the subjunctive on thought as upon a black boy in New Jersey.

It seems a tad absurd, upon which we must re-evaluate the initially seductive nature of statements such as *Languages evolve according to the needs of their speakers.* Quite simply, they do not. Of course languages develop new words for new things: that is as undeniable as it is uninteresting. However, beyond this, how a language is put together structurally has nothing to do with what its speakers need. Language is intriguing for countless other reasons.

Undercooked?

Of course no one has said that every element in a sentence has a Whorfian significance. However, as we pass through this one vibrant sentence of English, Whorfianism seems fraught no matter where we turn.

Cook seems innocent enough, but then English borrowed it from French—before which English, and its early Germanic kin like Old Norse, had no single generic word for cooking. One baked, roasted, boiled things—but there was no more one word for just cooking in general than today's English has one word that refers to both eating and drinking. (*Ingest*, technically, but it's highly formal—no one says *Man, I ingested too much meat and wine at Thanksgiving!*—and it applies more readily to solids than liquids: who ingests lemonade?)

Yet: if Russians see blue more vividly because they have separate words for dark blue and light blue, then we must explore whether modern English speakers perceive cookery less vividly than Iron Age villagers. What do we make of a notion that a Viking was more sensitive to distinctions in cooking techniques than today's foodie couple in San Francisco? Or, if the Jersey City schoolboy is less attuned to cooking techniques than Edward the Confessor, then he gave no evidence of it in his enthusiastic discussion of a future chicken dinner at eight in the morning.

Or is it that Whorfian effects are cancelled out by cultural developments that occur after a language has taken shape? If so, then how can we apply it to any human group? Languages are typically much more ancient than their current culture. They were often imposed on people beyond the ones they originated among: Arabic started as the language of an obscure group of nomads in Arabia and was only later imposed on Coptic-speaking Egyptians, Berber-speaking

North Africans, and others. Languages often change vastly over time anyway: Old English was much like German both in structure and vocabulary.

Which stage of language shapes the thoughts of speakers at which time—and then on top of that, exactly which kinds of thoughts, and why? Whorfianism must work harder on this kind of question to justify the implications many wish to draw from it.

* * *

Even humble little *it* has a story. Wouldn't English seem to have one more of its ducks in a row if it were *him, her, hit* rather than *him, her, it*? As a matter of fact that's the way it was in earlier English. However, *hit* was the only one of the three where eons of rapid pronunciation were so hard on the *h* that it truly wore away. With *him* and *her*, the *h* hangs on, although we say *'im* and *'er* as much as, if not more than, we actually enunciate *him* and *her*. However, in a sense modern English does have its ducks in a row in that in rapid speech, the little trio is properly *'im, 'er,* and *it*.

The Whorfian story of *it*, in contrast, requires insulting the Chinese again. In many languages, pronouns are highly optional when context can do the job—so much so that an English speaker might wonder how communication occurs. In Chinese, if someone asks *How'd you like the movie?* you can, and probably will, say back, *Didn't like* rather than *I didn't like it*. Japanese and many East and Southeast Asian languages are similar, as are countless ones worldwide. European languages like English are just prissier about getting that pronoun in there.

Does that mean our teen has a greater sensitivity to who is doing what to whom than a Chinese person? In deciding, we should also know that there are languages where to say *I met John* you have to include a redundant *him* as well: *I met-him John*. Is the African tribesman who speaks a language like that more aware of who is doing what to whom than a black boy in Jersey City?

Perhaps the tribesman's small, intimate social group conditions such an awareness? But what about the fact that equally small groups all over the world are just the kind of languages where you *don't* have to express pronouns? Random example: among the 2,500 Manambu of Papua New Guinea, actually overheard was someone saying, *If you feel like peeing, wake me up* as *Feel like peeing, wake*. After all, no one had any reason to think the person was referring to the urinary inclinations of the guy two doors down, much less that it would be useful to wake *him* up about one's own.

Thought is not the issue here. Language varies gorgeously astride the very *same* kinds of thoughts from group to group.

* * *

Too fast. Linguists and Whorfians, their thoughts perhaps shaped differently, will seize upon different things here.

The linguist sees how *fast* is like a feather. Feathers today aid birds' flight. They began as insulation and decoration on dinosaurs; for some, the feathers came to be of help in gliding, step by step over millions of years until what started as downy plumage on a *Compsognathus* became the aerodynamically splendid feathers of an eagle.

Fast, too, is the end stage of a process that began at quite a different point. Old English's word for *fast* was *snel*, just as

German's still is *schnell*. The word *fast* existed, but its meaning was firm, tight—as in a meaning it still has secondarily today: *hold it fast*. However, in this original meaning, one could say *run fast* in the meaning of running with tight application, vigorously, keeping at it. To run in such a fashion is, by definition, to be doing it quickly, and over time, that indeed became *fast's* main definition. Today the original meaning lurks in the margins, in words like *steadfast*, expressions like *stuck fast* and *fast asleep*, which if you think about it is kind of silly if fast means rapid—few sleepers sprint. *Fast asleep* hearkens back to when *fast* meant tight, tenaciously, which describes how quite a few of us do sleep (myself regrettably not among them).

In any language, most words have histories like this, starting quite distinctly from what we know them as, and having reached their current state via a stepwise development of inferences few are ever aware of within the span of a human life. *Quaint* first meant clever or crafty, and by extension, fashionable—note the remnant way we can still refer to a modishly dressed person as looking "smart." The extension continued over the years: the fashionable connotation acquired a negative air and sank into "elaborate," "affected." Time passed, and extension drifted into a more arch direction, from "affected" to our modern sense of quaint as "enticingly weird in an old-fashioned way." *Fast* is a case of this kind, perhaps even itself weird in an old-fashioned way.

But for Whorfianism, the potential meal in *too fast* is *too*. It is, for the record, an odder little word than we have reason to consider often. If asked, what would you say *too* meant? You might be surprised how much there would be to say. Have you ever learned a language in which there is a word referring both to addition (*me, too*) and excess (*too hot*)? In French, *aussi* but *trop*; in German, *auch* but *zu*; in Japanese, *mo* but *ammari*. Plus, *too* also has a specialized alternate meaning. In French, you deny a negation with *si* rather than a *oui*: Guillaume: *Tu n'as pas payé!* (You didn't pay!). Isabelle: *Si, j'ai payé!* (Yes I did pay!). German does the same thing with *Doch*, and an English speaker might wish we had such a thing—and we do. Craig: *You didn't do it.* Laura: *I did **too!***

One could consider these three meanings of *too* a neat little splotch; one never knows which related meanings one word might end up covering for various reasons. However, for Benjamin Lee Whorf, this kind of thing fell under the rubric of the "cryptotypes" that he thought of as the channels via which language shapes thought. One of his examples was that in Hopi, there is one word *masa'ytaka* for all things that fly except birds: such as insects, planes, pilots. There is also a different word for water occurring in nature as opposed to water that you cook with or drink. To Whorf this suggested that the Hopis' language conditioned them to process the world in ways that a language without these particular configurations would not.

Modern Whorfians are explicit in rejecting the more extreme claims of Whorf's writings. However, this is a matter of temperance; the basic orientation stays the same. No one today claims that languages prevent speakers from thinking in certain ways, or even make thinking in certain ways a strain; rather, we are to investigate whether languages make thinking in a particular way more likely. However, that likelihood is still treated as up for debate, and as such, the Hopis' classification of flying things and water is akin to work on, say, Russian words for blue. Moreover, Whorfian adherents outside of the academy are especially given to reading words' semantic spreads as indicative of weltanschauung. References to the Hopi *masa'ytaka* have been widespread and steady for eons now. Meanwhile, Mark Abley sees that French subdivides knowing between *savoir* for facts and *connaître* for people and supposes that "to a French speaker, that distinction is central to how the mind interacts with the world."

As such, *too* leads to a question. Let's say that *masa'ytaka* means that a people process flight as an especially vibrant distinguishing trait of moving objects, and that Europeans with their separate words for knowing people as opposed to knowing things have an insight into the contours of familiarity that others lack. If so, then when a word means "also," "overly," and "but I *did*!," what kind of interaction with the world does it condition?

The answer can't be that the things that *too* covers are too abstractly related to condition a way of thinking. After all, there is a short step from addition (*me, too*) to excess (*too much*), or from addition to refuting a denial by adding back the truth (*I did too!*). So: Do English speakers have a uniquely sensitive access to the concept of addition (*me, too*), as something potentially overdone (*too much*) but also useful in appending objections amid conversation (*I did too!*)? Many would not hesitate if such a claim were made about the Hopi as opposed to a lawyer in San Antonio, and one must admit that it's hardly more abstract than the idea that to be French is to carefully distinguish the knowing of a fact and the knowing of a person.

Yet in the end, let's suppose that in an experiment, our black adolescent in Jersey City could be shown to have a certain wisp of a readiness to associate addition, excess, and denial—a few milliseconds' more alertness to this peculiar squiggle of cognition than someone from Seoul. In the grand scheme of things, of all the ways that we might be interested in how American adolescents think, black or not, or how any Americans of any age think, or how English speakers worldwide think, what insight could this wee discovery about *too* lend us on issues humanistic, political, societal, artistic, educational, medical, or even psychological?

Anglerfish Testicles and the Future

I'm-a in Black English is an awesome little eddy of a thing, where *I am going to* has coalesced into what is essentially a single word. Imagine the extraterrestrial assigned to make sense of English who happened to come upon Black English first, learning only by ear and trying to figure out what people meant by this *I'm-a*—pronounced Ah-muh—when otherwise people are using *will* and *gonna* to indicate the future. *I'm-a* is very particular, not just a random instance of running words together. No one says "youra" for *you are going to* or "theya" for *they are going to*. The extraterrestrial, to be successful, would have to figure out that *I'm-a* is of all things something as specific as a *first-person singular future construction*. It's the kind of thing a person would often screw up on in an exam, if there were such a thing as Ebonics lessons.

It is one of those cluttered nodes that human languages can develop, seeming to almost willfully challenge those inclined to try unraveling them. French's *Qu'est-ce que c'est?* for *What is that?* is an example. Only because of the written convention can we parcel out that the expression is composed of *que, est, ce, que, ce* again and then *est* again—and we still wonder why French has all that just to ask *What's that?*

Just the *-a* part of *I'm-a* is rather gorgeous when we consider that it began as not one but two words, *going to. Going to* eroded to *gonna, 'onna,* and finally just *a,* as unlike its progenitor as French's *août,* pronounced just "oo," is like its Latin source *augustus.* The *-a* in *I'm-a* is the linguistic equivalent of the male anglerfish, tiny compared to the female, whose lifecycle consists of sucking onto the female's head permanently and gradually wearing away like a dying pimple until nothing is left but his testicles, whose sperm are absorbed into the female's bloodstream to fertilize her eggs! In *I'm-a, -a* is stuck to *I'm*'s forehead, fertilizing it with future meaning.

And then the *-m-* part of *I'm-a* is a shard of *am,* itself part of English's bizarrely multifarious community of *be*-verb forms. Irregular is one thing, but *am, are, is, be, been, was,* and *were* is a train wreck. The current situation is litter from no fewer than three different original verbs that collapsed together as if laughing together at a warmly potent joke, *beon, weson,* and *aron.* In any language, spots that undergo especial wear and tear tend to be messy—habit scorns logic. *Be* verbs are used a lot, and thus, like irregular plurals such as *man* and *men,* they tend not to be places to seek order. Thus the *-m-* in *I'm-a* and the *be* of *be eatin'* that the Jersey City boy used are two shards

from a three-verb traffic pileup that Germanic tribespeople allowed in early English two thousand years ago.

* * *

Meanwhile, recall that the Whorfian take on our adolescent's
future marker is that it will make him less likely to save
money.

* * *

As we near the end of the sentence, the message holds steady:
People think alike; it's the languages that change.

Does the guy's having a word for *eat* separate from one
meaning *drink* mean he likes food better than tribespeople
who have one word for both? It would be hard to say so when
earlier in the sentence his having a general word for *cook*
seemed to suggest on the contrary that he was less of a food
person than Hagar the Horrible.

When our teen says *some pink meat*, the *some* doesn't mean
"a little bit," but an extension of that meaning, suggesting a
diminution of its quality, a pejorative evaluation. All languages
have a way of conveying that flavor. Japanese would convey
the same attitude toward, say, pink meat with a collection of
words like *nante* and *nado*. In the Native American language
Klamath of the Pacific Northwest there was a prefix that did
the same job. There's always something.

Then, plenty of unwritten languages have words for only a
few colors, with *pink* certainly not one of them. In the 1960s at
the University of California at Berkeley, linguist-anthropologists
Brent Berlin and Paul Kay discovered that color terms emerge in
languages in a rough order. After black and white comes red,
then green and yellow, then blue, then brown, and only after

them, purple, pink, orange, and gray. That is, there is no such thing as a language with words for only black, yellow, and pink, or even black, white, and green.

In this light, it has been noted that Homer tossed off bizarre usages of color, such as references to not only wine-dark seas but wine-dark oxen, green honey, and blue hair. There was an early temptation to attribute this to Homer's reputed blindness, but then sighted Greeks were given to similar oddities, such as Euripides's green tears. Are we really to suppose that these hypersensitive artists did not see the colors we do?

The philosopher Empidocles gave the game away in dividing colors into what we process as an oddly spare palette: light, dark, red, and yellow. That is exactly what Berlin and Kay's flowchart predicts of a society that has yet to develop a prolific set of conventionalized terms for colors: black, white, red, and then yellow or green.

Yet Whorfian thought, with its Russian blues findings, teaches us to wonder whether the Ancient Greeks, as well as the peoples today with few color terms, actually processed color differently than we do. Does the Jersey City kid see pink flamingos and cherry blossoms as more distinctly un-red than Homer and Empidocles could have? Yet just as a difference of 124 milliseconds is hard to see as demonstrating a different way of seeing the world, it's hard to imagine that our Jersey City kid was imagining that pink meat he spoke of more "pinkly" than, say, Old English speakers would have perceived under-cooked meat, despite the fact that they didn't have a word for *pink* yet either.

At the end of our sentence not a single thing has seemed able to tell us much about how its speaker thinks. On *meat*, we might try the cryptotype route again: many African languages have the same word for both *animal* and *meat*. One may think first of people pointing to "meats" running around the savanna, but more properly, it's that these people see themselves as eating "animal." They do not make our prim distinction between living creatures and pieces of them sitting on our plate.

Is this a sign of a Western remove from the mundane reality that animal slaughter is required for our culinary delight? One is often taught so, in that English inherited from the French euphemistic distinctions like *beef* for cow on the plate and *pork* for pig on the plate. Now, truth be told, it would appear that this would classify as culture shaping language, not the other way around—but there is always the chicken and egg question, as well as the surmise that it might "go both ways."

As such, there is inconvenient data beyond France and Africa no matter how we approach the subject. Generally human groups do *not* have the same word for *animal* and *meat*. More typically, humans of all societal types have a word for animal flesh as distinct from the living animals. In fact, even Old English had this basic distinction between beasts and meat, despite the fact that its speakers tended to be much more intimately familiar with animal slaughter than anyone in Jersey City! It is, rather, the Africans in question among whom that particular bubble in the soup *happens* not to have burbled up, just as in English we do not *happen* to keep knowledge of people and knowledge of things separate.

What's Significant?

Dey try to cook it too fast, I'm-a be eatin' some pink meat! He said it. He was expressing a thought. And an attempt to Whorfian-ize it simply doesn't work. Not a single element in this boy's utterance can be scientifically identified as distinguishing how he thinks from how his Mongolian or Peruvian equivalent does.

An objection that my approach in this chapter caricatures Whorfianism is as implausible as it is likely. It would be hard to say that the sentence I used is unrepresentative of English or of normal thought. As casual and even humorous as it may be, it is language, pure and simple, replete with exactly the kinds of semantic and grammatical categories that have fascinated Whorfians since the Roosevelt administration. Hypothetical-ity, tense, color terms, classification of objects—it's all there. Might Whorfianism seem more intuitively applicable to that same sentence about the pink meat if it had been uttered by a farmer in the hills of Vietnam? It shouldn't: surely one need not be a Southeast Asian, Native American, or Amazonian to have a "worldview." Surely, that is, our Jersey City teen is a human being, with both thoughts and a language potentially shaping him.

Yet we have seen that it doesn't hold up that his specific way of experiencing life is channeled by how his language happens to play out. I must repeat: we can assume that English does have minute effects on his thought; on this, the data is in, from the best Whorfian experiments, as I acknowledged in chapter 1. My interest is in the implication drawn from this kind of work, partly by interested writers and partly by researchers themselves, that these perceptual differences amount to significantly different ways of experiencing existence.

"Who's to decide what's significant?" one rightly asks. Yet it must be clear, for example, that if English conditions a worldview, then that has to be a worldview that encompasses the frames of reference of that Jersey City boy, Mary Tyler Moore, Margaret Cho, William Jennings Bryan, and Sting. What's significant?—well, not whatever it is that unites the way those five people have processed life, I suspect most would agree. Clearly, that is a worldview so general as to be equivalent, essentially, to simply being human.

Is it that for some reason languages spoken as widely as English stop conditioning worldviews? For one, that would automatically disqualify Russian and Chinese from Whorfian experiments, as they are spoken by people of hundreds of distinct cultures. Yet, let's imagine a proposition that it's the "National Geographic" languages spoken by people of just one culture that shape thought. But why would language only shape thought among small groups? At what point in cultural development would we posit Whorfianism to peter out—and on what basis?

Besides, it's hard to see just how disqualifying big languages would work. Would the English someone speaks in New Delhi *not* condition a specifically English-conditioned worldview in her *because* English is also spoken in Sydney and Spokane? Surely the axiom cannot be "language shapes thought unless the language is spoken by different groups of people." The language in someone's head cannot "know" that it is spoken in heads on the other side of the world. Presumably a language shapes thoughts in whatever head it finds itself in.

One suspects that if anything is shaping a worldview for that English speaker in New Delhi, it is her specific culture, not how the verbs in the English she speaks—the same verbs used daily in London, Chicago, and Jersey City—work. Here, if we are seeking to glean some overarching sense in things—that is, to do science—it becomes attractive to suppose that culture is what shapes thought not only for the woman in New Delhi but also for the speaker of a local, obscure language. An analysis that covers everything, small languages and big ones, is that what shapes worldviews is culture, with how a people's grammar works having nothing significant to do with it. In the scientific sense, if language isn't shaping thought significantly on the streets of Jersey City, it isn't doing it in the Amazonian rain forest either.

* * *

Doing science indeed: Is science the bedrock of the almost narcotic appeal so many find in Whorfianism? One wonders. We are to think that the goal is simply the empirical one of investigating whether language shapes thought. Yet science never seems to quite seal the deal on this beyond tiny differentials gleaned from deeply artificial experiments. Recall that Guy Deutscher's *Through the Language Glass* is, properly speaking, a chronicle of the failure of a paradigm, yielding squeaks rather than peaks.

Notwithstanding, the media taught the reading public that his book investigated less whether language shapes thought than confirmed that it did so. And this was just a symptom of a general orientation: the media as well as academia continue to promulgate the idea that the question as to whether each language is a special pair of lenses is an open one. The very prospect of Whorfianism gets people going like a call to dinner.

Yet some Whorfianism goes over better than other Whorfianism. If Alfred Bloom had written a book claiming that Chinese makes its speakers *more* insightful in some ways than English speakers, he may well have won a Pulitzer.

There's a reason. It illuminates the core of Whorfianism's sexiness, and yet is also antithetical to an authentic and respectful exploration of the human condition.

CHAPTER 6

Respect for Humanity

THE VISCERAL APPEAL OF Whorfianism is not scientific.

Many will disagree, and the Neo-Whorfian researchers among them will do so with eminent justification. Neo-Whorfian researchers are, indeed, motivated by a scientific interest in the human mind. The question they pose is, quite simply, whether language influences thought, an issue with implications for broader ones, such as whether the capacity for language is embodied in the brain separately from other cognitive functions and the question as to which aspects of language might be the ones that affect thought.

However, that orientation to the question, one part clinical and one part philosophical, is not what lights up people beyond the small world of academic psychologists and anthropologists doing hard-core studies on Whorfianism. As I have noted, even among the originators of the paradigm, such as Benjamin Lee Whorf, his mentor Edward Sapir, and pioneering anthropologist Franz Boas, the main motivation of their observations about language and thought was to demonstrate that peoples we thought of as primitive were anything but. Whorf's aim in painting Hopi as channeling its speakers into feeling time as cyclical was not to detachedly assess whether language influences thought. Even a cursory reading of his works makes it radiantly clear that he had an agenda: to show that to be a Hopi was not to be a benighted savage.

That agenda was well intended and, in its time, urgent even among the intelligentsia. In Whorf's day, you could page through an edition of *Webster's Second New International Dictionary* and find Apaches casually described as "of warlike disposition and relatively low culture." The agenda is, in itself, hardly inapplicable today either—and is indeed fundamental to Whorfianism's place in today's intellectual culture, beyond the small circles of actual Neo-Whorfian practitioners. They themselves craft rigorous and uncompromisingly specific studies of fine points, often of languages spoken by people few dismiss as backward such as Russians and the Japanese.

But typically, today's sideline spectator, academic or not—in whom we might term the philosophy Popular Whorfianism—seeks in this work not a question as to whether language influences thought, but rather to a *demonstration* that all of the world's people are the mental equals of educated Westerners.

Advocacy or Reportage?

Of course it is rarely put that way. However, one indication is the bias in reception I have mentioned. The Whorfian study about a people's heightened sensitivity to the feel of materials or shades of a color is received as one more brick in the wall; the one using the same approach to suggest a deficiency in the

Chinese is diligently argued away. In the humanities, the same teacher who enthusiastically introduces undergrads to Whorf's idea as worth investigating may well have, in the same course, told students that it is mistaken to associate Black English's elisions of standard English grammar—such as often not using the *be* verb or third-person singular *-s*—with thought patterns. No teacher is being willfully obfuscatory here; I doubt any of them even have occasion to consider this particular contradiction. Yet it is instructive: the basic commitment is advocacy, not just investigation.

The advocational motivation is similarly clear not only in exchanges with people familiar with the Whorfian idea, but throughout the references to Whorfianism in journalistic and literary sources. Journalist Mark Abley listens to a Mohawk speaker talking about the word *ka'nikonriio* "righteousness." The speaker says, "You have different words. Something that is nice. Something coming very close to—sometimes used as a word for—law. The fact of *ka'nikonriio* is also 'beautiful.' Or 'good.' So goodness and the law are the same." Abley muses, "I had the impression that a three-hour philosophy seminar had just been compressed into a couple of minutes." Yet our own *righteous* has virtually the same spread of connotations, and one wonders whether Abley would see that as useful to discuss in a class about Kant and Hegel. Abley's aim here is not to show that language influences thought, but something more specific—that Mohawks *have* abstract thought just as English speakers do.

Journalist Jack Hitt describes an indigenous language of Chile called Kawesqar. It has several past tenses, including one that distinguishes the mythological from the real. Cool—but then Hitt surmises that Kawesqar barely marks the future because as former nomads, they apparently had lived largely in the moment and hadn't needed to think much about the future. The future tense seems to really get people's creative juices going when it comes to Whorfianism: recall Keith Chen treating it as discouraging—not encouraging—thrift, while literary critic Edmund Wilson thought Russian's ambiguous future marking was why Russians seemed never to be on time! Hitt's contribution here, just as creative, is more than a matter of showing a link between language and thought. The idea of a people too immersed in the moment to concern themselves with an abstract and uncontrollable later-on is romantic, a direct descendant of Whorf's depiction of the Hopi. Hitt's message is "These people make *sense*." He is clear on this: "Every language has its unique theology and philosophy buried in its very sinews."

Examples continue, such as K. David Harrison's idea that languages are testaments to ingenuity. Or, Daniel Everett's work on Pirahã is founded on an argument that particularities of their language, of which the numberlessness is but one, demonstrate a close evolutionary adaptation to their environment, analogous to physical ones. These people are not savages—they make *sense*.

In general, anyone familiar with the culture of academic social science will recognize a highly prevalent indignation at the notion of anyone implying that language and culture can be separated—a strain of thought that even motivated my third chapter. And of course even to those in the bleachers on such things, it may seem obvious that language and culture are related. However, one might ask: Why *indignation*, specifically, at the possibility that someone denies it?

Imagine someone denying that hydrogen and oxygen are the components of water—it's tough to envision the response being along the pearl-clutching lines of "How *dare* he!" Clearly there is something extra that conditions this subjective kind of response about language and culture, something as emotional as intellectual. Namely, the interest is less in showing that language is related to what a people are like, than in showing that language is related to why a people *should be liked*.

That is, we are to value not just how languages demonstrate a people's culture, but how their cultures are legitimate and sophisticated. Naturally, then, to people of the persuasion in question, the very prospect of dissociating language from what is good about people strikes them not only as mistaken, but as dismissive, irritating, offensive.

And one might well ask what is wrong with seeking to illuminate the good in as many people on earth as possible. It's positive, tolerant, enlightened—wouldn't it be behind the curve to resist such a thing? Abley and Hitt, for instance, have been committed to keeping obscure languages from going extinct. K. David Harrison seeks to keep indigenous cultures alive. Surely celebrating their speakers is relevant to that mission. They and countless others have the best of intentions.

I suggest, nevertheless, that the conventional embrace of Whorfianism, with its particular brand of elevating the particular over the universal, takes good intentions in directions none could favor. There are three goals Whorfianism seeks that are, unwittingly, subverted amid its typical treatments in public discussion.

Problem One—Honesty

Are Worldviews Always Noble?

The literature on the worldviews that languages create elides that if the analysis is correct, there are some distinctly unsavory aspects of the worldviews in question. To fashion an idea that a language can make you feel more or see more requires that one also accept that a language can also make you, for example, more racist or sexist.

Note that I did not write that "language" in general can be racist or sexist, something obvious to all. In any language one can produce sentences that have racist or sexist meaning. Deciding how to approach that is a subject separate from that of whether a given language in itself has a racist or sexist substrate—and some do.

Many are well aware that Romance and Germanic languages familiar to us are among them. We are taught that while in the singular, English distinguishes *he* from *she*, in the plural *they* is to be understood as referring to both genders. However, experiments have shown that as we might expect, the default tendency is to associate supposedly gender-neutral pronouns with men. The naked sexism built into the very grammar of such languages is clearer in languages like French, in which there actually is a third-person plural pronoun referring to women, *elles*, but when referring to both genders, the male *ils* is used, which is even the very word for *he* pluralized, as if to really rub it in. Imagine if in English one said of a group composed of men and women as "He-s are going upstairs shortly." (Yes, graphically *he* is contained within the word *they* as the letters *h* and *e*, but only accidentally; the *h* comes for free with the *t* to indicate the *th* sound.)

The problem is that this kind of casual sexism is built into languages around the world, as a sadly strong tendency among human groups. It gets even more immediate. The Native American language Koasati is very much of the kind that is full to bursting with fine-grained grammatical distinctions that would lend themselves to speculations as to whether a Koasati is more attuned to, basically, life as we know it. However, among those distinctions is one between whether one is a man speaking or a woman. Men speak with an extra suffix. If a woman says, "He's lifting it" she says *lakáw*, but if a man says it, it's *lakáws*. "You are saying"—for a woman, *ísk*, for a man, *ísks*. This distinction runs throughout the verbal system. In the language of India Kũrux, there are special endings for women talking to women, as opposed to the "normal" ones for men talking to men—or women!

Languages can also be what Westerners would term racist. The Native American language Yuchi, apart from all of its splendiferous busy-ness, has special pronouns to refer to Yuchis, as opposed to the other set used for everybody else. There is perhaps a tendency to see this as a kind of salutary self-regard in a small group like this, but then we would likely see it as quite different if, say, German or Chinese worked that way.

To these things, a tempting reaction is to doubt that these features condition a "worldview." But short of a metric that justifies fencing off sexism and racism from other aspects of a worldview, one is required to classify the other bells and whistles in a language as equally unrelated to how its speakers see the world.

There is some support for that position, in fact. There do exist languages in which the feminine, rather than the masculine, is the default. In them, more words are feminine than masculine, a new word created or brought into the language is spontaneously marked feminine, and/or when there are males and females present, it's the feminine pronoun that is used. For one, they are the exceptions that prove the rule, very rare—as it happens, the Amazonian Jarawara we keep hearing about in this book, and sister societies to theirs, are examples.

Second, however, we search in vain for evidence that these societies cherish women in an instructive way. Rather, the treatment of women in such societies seems almost counterintuitively incommensurate with a grammar that gives preference to the feminine gender. Among one of these groups, the Banawá, when a girl menstruates for the first time she is confined to a hut for months, only allowed out for excretion and bathing, in which case a basket is woven tightly around her head without even eye slits; when she is released, after an extended celebration she is beaten on the back until bloody.

Most certainly in this case, language is not creating a worldview in any way we would recognize. Popular Whorfianism would rather not dwell on such a thing—which could shed light on the broader Whorfian approach to other things a language supposedly makes its speakers meaningfully sensitized to.

Problem Two—Respect

Through the Microscope

Whorfianism, in the guise the public is encouraged to embrace, is condescension.

That's the last thing intended, and many promulgators would consider themselves seeking to make us simply see obscure peoples as Westerners' equals. They cherish diversity and want to spread the word. However, the idea that language is interesting because it shows how diverse we are as souls is neither as inevitable a perspective as it seems, nor as automatically benevolent.

This is easy to see from Whorfianism's earlier place in intellectual culture. Let us recall dear old Prussian Heinrich von Treitschke, with his "differences of language inevitably imply differing outlooks on the world." One does not imagine the most charitable view of languages beyond those spoken in geopolitically dominant nations, and indeed, von Treitschke's terms for the less fortunate peoples of the world was "barbarians," among whom were included not only obscure Third Worlders but groups close to home such as Lithuanians. In von Treitschke's Germanophone world not long before, even as erudite a philosopher-linguist as Wilhelm von Humboldt treated Chinese, with its lack of gender and conjugation endings, as representing an earlier "stage" of language than European ones, unsuitable to the highest degrees of reasoning and progress. The title of one of his signature works says it all: "The Diversity of Human Language-Structure and its Influence on the Mental Development of Mankind." The distance is short between this and the modern quest to show languages as "worldviews"—not for nothing is von Humboldt even classified by some as the true father of Whorfianism.

We consider ourselves blissfully beyond this kind of thinking. For one, modern Whorfians do not situate languages on a scale of sophistication the way the old-timers did, and such a quest is certainly the last thing on the minds of Whorfians' supporters even beyond academia.

Or is it? Von Humboldt seems so antique in his interest in "the mental development of mankind" (perhaps even more so in the original: *die geistige Entwicklung des Menschengeschlects*). However, even today, diversity is properly too general a term for how Whorfianism is argued for. Aspects of the diversity that would strike us as unpleasant are carefully pruned out of the picture, such as the sexism and racism aforementioned, or the possibility that a language makes you less sensitive to the hypothetical (Chinese), or things that significantly never come up for discussion, such as languages that collapse *eat* and *drink* into a word meaning *consume*. Rather, the dominant impulse of popular Whorfianism is to show ways in which other groups are Westerners' superiors: more aware of kinds of knowing, less caught up in obsessing about the future, more aware of their topography, more sensitive to sources of information.

The English speaker just talks; the Mohawk speaks philosophy lessons. The indigenous language is a testament to creativity—but those who would espouse that view are much less likely to write about English that way. To them, the doughty, donnish tradition of singing English as a "mighty" language is distant, old-fashioned, and redolent of imperialism. Under that perspective, slang does qualify as "creative"—but the approval stems from slang's flouting the musty tropes of the standard English hegemon. The Aboriginal Australian languages will be said to have no word for time, reflecting their conception that progress does not happen and that humans' job is to maintain life as it was at the Creation—and that hence, such people could never have driven the world to its global warming and other ecological problems.

For whatever it's worth, plenty of Australian languages have had a word for time, but that one and the others suffice to make a case—that would be supported by endless other statements by people on the relationship of language and culture—that there is more afoot than a celebration of diversity. In the quest to dissuade the public from cultural myopia, this kind of thinking has veered into exotification. The starting point is, without a doubt, *I respect that you are not like me.* However, in a sociocultural context in which that respect is processed as intellectually and morally enlightened, inevitably to harbor that respect comes to be associated with what it is to do right and to be right as a person. An ideological mission creep thus sets in: respect will magnify into something more active and passionate. The new watch cry becomes:

*I **like** that you are not like me.*
or alternately:
What I like about you is that you are not like me.
That watch cry signifies:
What's good about you is that you are not like me.

Note, however, the object of that encomium has little reason to feel genuinely praised. His being not like a Westerner is neither what he feels as his personhood or self-worth nor what we should consider it to be, either explicitly or implicitly. Ultimately, our characterization of indigenous people in this fashion is more for our own benefit than theirs. This is visible in that the person who elevates cherishing the values and folkways of others as more "real" than their own typically has no such expectations of the people in question.

The idea is that the "exotic," if he sees his people as superior to or more fundamental than us, is on the right track—kudos to him for understanding that we are the weirdos, the unenlightened, the uncool. But that is something we value for its validation of us, which we walk away with without considering that we are granting him a perspective we consider backward in ourselves. To wit, we celebrate him for being backward. That is no compliment.

Quite simply, we might imagine being on the other end of the microscope. A group of people observes what we do—including how we talk—and is entranced by the very fact of our differences from them, even elevating them as in some way more "genuine" than their own. Perhaps the narrative trope of our being observed and visited by extraterrestrials advanced far beyond us technologically is a useful comparison, with the unaccustomed sensation of smallness and trivialization a reader experiences. Take the analogy further and imagine the extraterrestrials praising how "real" we are for still living on the resources of our planet rather than channeling energy from some interplanetary source, and so on.

To scorn diversity is antithetical to egalitarianism. However, to fetishize it, while perhaps seeming progressive, can be equally elitist. Do we celebrate people as interesting in studied ways—"Wow, you really *feel* the length and thinness of sticks!"; "Gee, you're really *hip* to the difference between whether you saw something or only heard it!"—ultimately because we can't quite feel that they are our equals just in being human?

Problem Three—Accuracy

What Is Enlightenment?

Popular Whorfianism—we need a delineating term—just isn't true. Academic Neo-Whorfianism is—make no mistake. But how it is commonly interpreted beyond the laboratory just isn't real.

Language does not shape thought in the way that one might reasonably suppose, nor do cultural patterns shape the way language is structured in the way that one might reasonably suppose. Rather, the way a language is structured is a fortuitously ingrown capacity. It is a conglomeration of densely interacting subsystems, wielded at great speed below the level of consciousness, endlessly morphing into new sounds and structures due to wear and tear and accreted misinterpretations, such that one day what was once Latin is now French and Portuguese.

This conception must not be equated with the Chomskyan idea that a "language organ" exists distinct from the rest of cognition. All indications are that language is a component of thinking, and as such, this thing called language, engulfed in a perceiving brain, is ever tossing out feelers into various areas of conception—randomly, as there are so very many things a language might end up marking explicitly and no one could ever mark all of them—a dazzling thousands of facets of being human.

However, the perception capacity itself is the same regardless of the language. To be sure, a feeler, hooked into a certain patch of perception, enhances the speaker's sensitivity to the relevant phenomenon, and this book in no way denies the solid evidence for that. Yet the experiments in question have shown us that the enhancement qualifies as a passing flicker, that only painstaking experiment can reveal, in no way creating a *different way of seeing the world* along the lines that a von Humboldt, von Treitschke, or anyone else would propose.

As such, culture—the sum of how a people think—cannot permeate the glutinous nucleus that is how a language works. Note, I write how *a* language *works*, not just "language," which, as I have shown, is certainly affected by culture in various ways. Our interest—because it is Whorfianism's—is not just "language" writ large, but the fortuitous conglomeration that is the inner workings of an individual language—its grammar, how it happens to render *last week*, the particularities that make it tough to pick up by adults. Culture can affect how that language is used and make it label certain things that the culture values most in a fashion none would consider mysterious. However, culture cannot affect anything as integral to the language as how it is built in its details. A language's structure, and what random aspects of reality it happens to cover or not cover, do not correlate meaningfully with culture.

Yes: *language structure does not correlate meaningfully with culture.* You don't need to take my word for it. Just as Edward Sapir told us almost a century ago, "When it comes to linguistic form, Plato walks with the Macedonian swineherd, Confucius with the head-hunting savage of Assam." The vocabulary is awkward today, but Sapir meant that the Macedonian language, related to Russian, is bristling with cases and conjugations just like Ancient Greek, while Chinese is built like various small languages spoken in South and Southeast Asia. Culture and language structure—that is, thought and language structure—do not match. That is a message perhaps unexpected from one of the figures who inspired Whorf, but there it is. This is what we have seen in this book.

In the light of it, how comfortable can we be with celebrating small languages' vocabularies as "embodying a cultural perspective"? After all, it is so clear that the vocabularies of our own languages are, well, just words. Spanish has separate words for a corner depending on whether it's outside (you go around the *esquina*) or inside (you stand in the *rincón*). English has the same word for both, but few consider that to embody a "geometry lesson"—English just happens to cut up reality in a randomly different way than Spanish. French doesn't have a word for *stick out* in the sense of something being improperly placed within an otherwise tidy row of objects but imagine French scientists deciding that this means that English's *stick out* means that we are culturally more attuned to things protruding than they are! The French just happen to express the concept as a matter of something not having been done right, or something "going beyond" (*dépasser*); they get the meaning across even if they don't have a word that happens to incorporate that "sticking" nuance.

No language's words can mark every single nuance of living, and thus every language happens to divide conception up differently. The differences are neat, but the idea that they indicate different takes on life is valid only to the extent that we can accept it about languages close to home. If despite their language Swedes wipe and the French can see things sticking out, then the whole picture we are often given about indigenous vocabularies falls apart.

* * *

The scholar who studies the works of Saint Thomas Aquinas readily allows that as brilliant a thinker as he was, much of what he wrote about cannot much occupy the modern mind, such as his endless disquisitions on the Aristotelian difference between the essential and the accidental properties of objects, with the latter kind carefully taxonomized, all in the service of parsing theological questions revolving around transubstantiation and the Eucharist. One can put oneself into Saint Thomas Aquinas's mind and understand the urgency such issues had to him in the thirteenth century, while still feeling that this stage of philosophical investigation was couched in certain assumptions and preoccupations that modern philosophy, amid the progress of intellectual history, has surpassed in terms of empiricism.

Similarly we can thoroughly understand why even the most scientific of minds once believed in spontaneous generation. It certainly looked as if life could spring from putrid matter, and only with microscopes and rigorously wielded deductive tools could humans perceive microorganisms.

The study of language has had similar phases, which, in retrospect, seem understandable but primordial. If you only know of languages that have a lot of endings that have to be learned via busy-looking tables, it is natural to think a language that lacks these is less sophisticated, as Wilhelm von Humboldt did. Only with extended study of languages like Chinese does it become clear that endings are hardly the only way that a language can be difficult (as I try to show in my book *What Language Is*), and even today the layman is given to saying that languages like Chinese "don't have grammar."

Equally germane here would be the quaint von Treitschkes of yore with their idea that languages represent how people think. The reader likely can see where I'm going: the idea that each language makes its speakers think differently—even in a "good" way—from speakers of others is perhaps not as progressive as it appears. One clue is in the very fragility immediately evident in the idea that all of the differences will be good, or even "cool." We have seen the problem, and must add that the school of thought is typically based on a tiny base of comparison—two to four languages out of six thousand—such that one is forced into a comparison similar to blind men describing an elephant.

One could say, then, that popular Whorfianism, for all of its sincerely beneficent intentions, is an immature position, a stage along the pathway toward treating language as what it actually is, a stage in which we are deeply preoccupied by concerns local to our moment, which, in their visceral pull, discourage attention to the larger picture. The analogy with Saint Thomas Aquinas's writings could continue, in that just as religious commitments diverted him from what modern philosophers would consider a purely empirical approach, the modern popular Whorfian enthusiasm is rooted in what could be termed a religious impulse as well, that is, the modern thinking person's allegiance to valuing, fostering, and defending diversity rather than disparaging it.

That is, a "religion" that has vastly improved human societies in inestimable ways. However, as I have argued, when it comes to how a given language works, this religion all but inevitably drifts into an essentialism antithetical to anything most would see as looking ahead, pardoning the lesser, and celebrating the ordinary, all in the name of a validation that its object would barely recognize.

Popular Whorfianism is hardly the only symptom of a slip between folk consciousness and the empirical when it comes to language. Prescriptivism—the idea that there are "bad" grammatical forms, mistaken in some scientifically unexceptionable way—is another. One aspect of being a linguist is an eternal crusade against the folk notion that it is "broken" to say *Billy and **me** went to the store; Each student can hand in **their*** *paper*; or *There were **less** books there than I thought*. The idea that such locutions are "wrong," while so widespread and thus so seemingly plausible, is rooted in fiats laid down centuries ago by men learned but of limited linguistic horizons, thinking that English should pattern like Latin, or equating linguistic logic with mathematical logic regardless of whether linguistic logic accomplishes its goal of conveying meaning accurately. The linguist awaits the day when the general public will understand that the prescriptivism we are raised on is based on illusory commandments that have no scientific basis.

Many adherents of popular Whorfianism are of one mind with linguists on that, but miss that the general public is equally misled in thinking that if Western European languages have different words for knowing depending on whether it's factual (French *savoir*, German *wissen*) or acquaintance (French *connaître*, German *kennen*), then it means speakers of those languages are keener about what it is to know than English speakers are. Or, they miss that the general public is ill served to be taught that indigenous groups that have to use a suffix to say where they got their information from are keener on what it is to know their environment than other people are. The very idea is so cool, but in the grand scheme of things just doesn't hold up. Recall—do we really think that Africans, who rarely have such suffixes, *don't* need to be alert to nuances of their environment?

Is our perspective on language to progress beyond its current stage? Is the public's enlightenment on language to increase via the teachings of our writerly class in the way that Immanuel Kant hoped thought would progress in his classic piece, "What Is Enlightenment?" If so, here is the kind of siren call we must reconsider.

English, as it happens, has a *get* fetish. Asked what *get* means, we most readily say that it means to acquire. But the word has seeped throughout the language far beyond that. To understand something is to *get* it. To overcome something by force is to *get* it—I'm going to *get* you. To enter into some state is to *get* that way. You *get* someone to do something. You *get* to go to the ball. You even *get* fired, *get* hurt.

The possibility beckons to treat this as evidence of something about being an English speaker. An academic so inclined might phrase it that these meanings of *get* suggest a revealing ethnosemantic reality, in which English speakers express a fundamental cultural orientation via their particular usage of what seems, on the surface, an unremarkable little word.

Linguist Anna Wierzbicka, as it happens, actually has had an idea of this kind. She points out that sentences like *She got him to do it*, *She got mad*, and *She got herself kicked out* all carry an implication that someone has undergone something without having intended to. She sees this as a result of democracy of all things, under which "the new managerial type of society" needed "an increased scale of interpersonal causations," under which a language might distinguish nuances such as whether or not something was caused with the intent of the person undergoing the causing. She also supposes that democracy's forging of a cultural focus on personal autonomy—or its suppression—further encouraged the florescence of these kinds of *get* constructions.

In arguments such as these, Wierzbicka is often thought to have shown, without falling for the cartoonier renditions of

Whorfianism, that even English can teach us how language reflects culture. She deserves credit for venturing to do that, in contrast to the more usual disinterest I pointed to in chapter 4 in how our own familiar English "shapes thought." But as insightful as she often is, her conclusions are based largely on a few languages spoken in Europe. Surely we need a bigger sample to determine whether English's *get* fetish has to do with being "Anglo-Saxon" or even "Anglo," as she often puts it, as opposed to simple chance.

There are, as it happens, dozens of languages in Southeast Asia spoken by small, indigenous groups, living according to agrarian traditions tracing back millennia, in which *get* has slipped beyond its borders and permeated the languages similarly to the way it has in English. In tiny languages like Muong, Alak, Brao, and Zhuang, one not only *gets* a present from someone. When one must go home, one "gets" home; if you can dance, you "get" dance; if you are a slow walker, then one would say that you are someone who "gets" walking slow; if you laugh so hard your sides ache, then your laugh "gets" your sides aching. Notably, most of these meanings entail someone undergoing something unexpectedly or unwillingly, just as the English *get* constructions do.

And then, this *get* proliferation is also rife in the "star" languages of the area like Thai, Vietnamese, and Lao, which have entirely different histories from the obscure ones. Knowing only about the *get* fetish in well-known languages like Thai, we might suppose that the commercial and cultural dominance of these people had something to do with their enshrinement of the word for acquire, along the lines of what supposedly happened in England. Yet the obscure languages off in the hills, also as *get*-crazy as English, sit as a block on making any kind of Whorfian sense of the matter.

The only coherent account is that all of these languages *got* the way they are by chance. They extended a feeler into *get*-ness, rather than evidentiality, or having different words for dark blue and light blue, or different words for eating depending on what's in your mouth. You never know where in the soup a bubble may come up—and ladies and gentleman, that's all.

Similarly, when journalist Amy Wilentz insightfully describes how the unfortunate history of Haiti has necessitated a tradition of artful dissimulation in the local culture, but then treats Haitian Creole's using the same word for *he*, *she*, and *it* and the same word for *we* and *you all* as its linguistic symptom, it is a reasonable supposition. However, it also isn't true: the correlation is an accident.

Chinese and Finnish have all-purpose *he*, *she*, *it* pronouns despite their nations' pasts and presents being so different from Haiti's. Meanwhile many locales as historically troubled as Haiti have pronouns that slice up reality even more finely than English's do, such as many languages of the South Seas area that have different words for me and you, me and you and him, and me and you and them, where English just has *we*.

And as to the same pronoun for *we* and *you all*, Haitian gets that from the African language spoken by many of its creators three hundred years ago. There is no anthropological analysis of those people, the Fon of Benin, as having a culture based on disguise and indirection—they are an indigenous culture tracing back several millennia, which birthed its fuzzy pronouns unconnected to the exigencies of plantation slavery. Their pronouns for *we* and *you all* just happened to end up the same—just as in merrie Old England for a while, as we saw in the previous chapter, for a while *he* and *they* were the same word. No one thinks that had anything to do with British peasants tossing up crafty linguistic smoke screens; it just happened because that's what languages fall into now and then as sounds wear away and lead to homonyms. Just homonyms—all languages have them, and if English's homonymy between *May* and *may* just "is," then the burden is upon Whorfians to explain why the homonymy between Haitian's *nou* "we" and *nou* "y'all" is "cultural."

Haitian's pronouns have nothing to do with the culture of Haitians. It only seems so with the camera pulled in to view only Haitian Creole and a few languages we happen to know best. Wilentz, to be sure, cannot be faulted for not knowing this. She is a top-rate journalist with no pretenses of being a linguist and has simply taken in the Whorfian current that educated people in our times do. Only linguists have any reason to be familiar with language as it patterns worldwide. If a people are hanging garlic in a doorway to ward off colds, it is the medical establishment's fault for not disseminating the truth. In the same way, popular Whorfian insights like Wilentz's are not her fault.

It is linguists, anthropologists, and psychologists who are responsible for enlightening the public that language does not track with culture the way we might expect it to. If empiricism remains eternally our goal, it is relevant that language can remain an inspiring thing without the distortions of popular

Whorfianism. We can, retaining a quest for enlightenment, move ahead.

The Wonders of Sameness

The truth is that language dances only ever so lightly on thought. One proof of this is how terminology's meanings quickly bend according to thought patterns. University of California linguist George Lakoff, for example, has notoriously suggested that the Democratic Party could attract more voters by altering the labels they apply to things of political import, such as calling income taxes "membership fees" and trial lawyers "public-protection attorneys." Lakoff's idea has seemed less urgent since the Barack Obama phenomenon created a Democratic ascendance on its own, but the idea could have had at best a temporary impact. Terminology doesn't shape thought, it follows it.

Consider terms such as *affirmative action*, now so conventional we rarely stop to parse what the actual words composing it mean: "affirming" what? What kind of "action"? The term was artful and gracious, giving a constructive, positive air to an always controversial policy. Note, however, that political opponents soon came to associate the term with the same negative feelings they had about the policy it referred to, such that today it is uttered with scorn by many. *Welfare* is similar. The contrast between the core meaning of the word and its modern political associations is instructive, in that one can easily imagine a Lakoff in the 1930s proposing exactly the word *welfare* as a label for government assistance. Notably, another term of art for the same policy, *home relief*, rapidly took on the same kinds of negative associations. Similarly, if an issue commonly attracts dismissive attitudes, those regularly accrete to any new terms applied. This happened quickly to urgently intended terms such as *male chauvinist* and *women's liberation*, as well as *special education*.

Changing the terms can play some initial role in moving opinion, rather like God getting the globe spinning under the deist philosophy. But what really creates change is argumentation, as well as necessary political theatrics. Mere terms require constant renewal as opponents quickly "see through" the artful intentions of the latest ones coined and cover up the old label with the new one, applying it to the attitudes they have always had. Only in an unimaginably totalitarian context that so limited the information available to citizens that constructive thought and imagination were near impossibilities could language drive culture in a *lasting* way. This is why Orwell and *1984*, expected references at this point in my discussion, are not truly relevant here. In the real world, language talks about the culture; it cannot create it.

Rather than each revealing a different take on thinking, languages—beyond having names for cultural tokens—are variations on the same take on thinking: the human one. This may sound unexciting, but homogeneity can be more interesting than it sounds. Its very prevalence among humans is as much a lesson, in terms of the counterintuitive, as diversity.

Anthropologist Donald Brown's catalog of human universals is invaluable here. It will surprise few that all humans have art or use tools. However, many of the things that have been found in all human groups worldwide are not what one would expect, and make one feel part of a species defined by much more than physiognomy and the infant's instinct to cry. For example, in all groups there is an equivalent to marriage; nowhere do people engage solely in informal sexual arrangements. All humans have a particular fear of snakes. All groups have a kind of music associated with children and child care. There is no human group that does not indulge occasionally in some kind of stimulant or intoxicant. The facial expressions a woman makes when flirting are the same the world over. To consider excretion and sex private acts is not solely a Western "hangup," but is found among all human beings anywhere. Linguistically, some languages say "not good" for bad, "not wide" for narrow, and so on, but none have *negative* terms as the default for basic concepts like these: no language has "not bad" for good, "not narrow" for wide.

Another example is one of my favorites. The speakers of the creole language Saramaccan in the Surinamese rain forest that I mentioned previously create, as all humans do, art. Collectors have valued their baskets, textiles, and woodcarvings, thinking of them as testaments to age-old indigenous tradition. We imagine the Saramaka passing the same artistic patterns down one generation after another, such that today's carver is carrying on the tradition of his distant ancestors in seventeenth-century Surinam, when the society formed.

Yet nothing could be further from the truth. Surinam's artists, while thoroughly immersed in respect for their ancestors, are no more interested in cranking out the same patterns year after year than anyone else. Among them, just as with any sculptor in Paris or Los Angeles, art changes throughout a lifetime and over generations. To them, a basket weaved a hundred years ago is instantly identifiable as old-fashioned, and not something any weaver would make today.

A Surinam artist told an anthropologist, after mentioning the constant novelty in the West,

> Well, friend, it's exactly the same with our woodcarving! My uncle's generation only knew how to make those big, crude designs—the one we call "owl's eyes" and "jaguar's eyes"—but since then men have never stopped making improvements. Almost every year there's something new, something better. Right up to today.

The men are also rather irritated by Western collectors' notion that their work must have quaint or exotic "meanings" about things like fertility or eternal dualities. To them, their artworks are ... art, fashioned the way it is out of the basic human creative impulse.

Things like Brown's universals and Surinamese art show us, then, that diversity is not the only way that humans can be interesting. Surely part of embracing diversity is understanding the extent of homogeneity in which it occurs.

Then Isn't Language Boring?

Language demonstrates this homogeneity quite vibrantly. Some may find this proposition less enticing, less romantic, less interesting than the Whorfian one. In fact, part of what detours us into the idea that each language is a different worldview is likely that otherwise, an element of the romantic is lost.

For example: one hears often that "When I speak (language X), I'm a different person!" Yet it isn't an accident that people who say this almost always learned that language as adults. The reason they are "different" in the second language is that they don't speak it natively! It follows naturally that if you probe a bit and ask the person to describe how they are different in the second language, they usually say they aren't as witty or are more blunt—that is, just what one expects from someone who is fluent but not native.

Yet there is wonder in how languages are different nevertheless—in how very differently languages express the same basic cognitive process called humanity. It cannot be denied that some languages pack more observation into the typical sentence than others: the difference between what a typical Native American language requires you to say and what a typical Mandarin Chinese sentence does is obvious. However, in any language one can, if necessary, say anything, and it is miraculous to observe how variantly languages accomplish this possibility.

For example, here is an English sentence:

Should we make them help to take it away?

Now, in a language called Lahu, spoken in villages in southern China and nearby countries, the way you would put this is:

We help take go send give correct yes?

Lahu, like Chinese, is one of those languages without endings, of the kind one easily supposes therefore to not have "grammar." In Lahu we see (or hear) just short words strung together like beads: *ŋàh i ga yù qay c i pî cô ve lâ*?

It seems especially unlike anything we know as grammar that so much of the Lahu sentence is verbs just run together like train cars: help-take-go-send-give-correct—how in the world does that mean "should help them to take it away"?

But it does, very precisely. Where English uses "little words" like articles and prepositions, Lahu instead makes rich use of verbs in secondary meanings. "Go" means "away." "Send" means "make" as in putting them forth for a purpose—you can feel how *send them to* could come to mean *make them to* just as in English, *see* can be used in the sentence *See that they take it away.* "Give" indicates that the sending—that is, the making— is directed toward someone, and as an indication of how languages can hide their grammar, this word for *give* is used only in the third person and therefore also, "for free," signifies to a Lahu that we are making *them*, rather than me or you. That is, this sentence does have an indication of *them*—just not where we would ever know to look. "Correct," extended in a similar way as *send* to *make*, means "should."

Lahu is full of surprises. The final "yes" is not a random affectation, and my translation is even loose—really, it's a word you must append to indicate that something is a question: more grammar, directly equivalent to English's inverting *we* and *should* to indicate the same thing (*Should we . . .?*). And finally, in the translation I left out notoriously untranslatable little *ve* that comes after all of the verbs. Its function is so elusive that the world's expert on the language, my erstwhile colleague Jim Matisoff, wrote an article on its complexities perfectly titled "Oy, ve!" But, basically, in Lahu putting forth a question involves rendering it all as a kind of gerund, rather like an Israeli I once knew who, new to English, once offered cigarettes to friends asking, "Smoking?" instead of "Want to smoke?" In Lahu, the sentence in question comes out as roughly, "Us being obliged to make them help take it away, hmm?" Now, there's some grammar, as arbitrary as the fact that in English *should* is irregular.

Lahu, then, is interesting in how it expresses the same thoughts as English does, but with such vastly different machinery. If Lahu were endangered, which luckily it is not at present, the fact that it is so awesome simply in itself would be justification for at least documenting what it is.

Yet more likely in our modern zeitgeist is a claim that Lahu is valuable as a window on a way of seeing the world—that it embodies a worldview from the way its sentences work. Here, we are back to the kinds of things we have seen in this book: Lahu has the material classifiers like Chinese and Japanese, it has an evidential marker or two, and so forth. Yet at the end of the day, a notion that Lahu grammar shapes a way of thinking would lead us down blind alleys familiar to the reader by now. We need not even linger on the ultimately patronizing idea that Lahu's stringing verbs together rather than using prepositions and adverbs means that its speakers are more "active," "vivid," or "direct" than English speakers. Or, Lahu doesn't really mark past tense: so if not marking the future means you save more money, then maybe the Lahu attend *more* to the past than other people? Or, just as Japanese uses the same classifier for pencils, beer, and phone calls, Lahu uses the same one for months and testicles—it'd be interesting figuring out what that might say about the Lahu as a people.

And so it would go. Lahu grammar is a marvelously intricate system in its own right. Is part of what delineates a culture *the fact of* having a language unique to it? Certainly. However, from that, it does not follow that the language is the culture couched as sentence patterns and word groupings. In its relationship to the essence and particularities of a culture, how a language works is analogous to a tartan.

What Is Forward?

There are those for whom a statement like that just will not do. They may marvel that someone who has written with such enthusiasm about the variety among the world's languages in books such as *The Power of Babel* and *What Language Is* could deny the intimate relationship between language and culture.

However, this book is perfectly compatible with those. I deny not that language and culture are linked. I question a particular kind of linkage between the two, in which grammatical features and vocabulary configurations no native speaker would consider at all remarkable purportedly condition a way of processing life. To question that idea is neither to toss one's hat in with the Chomskyans reducing language to a spare little clot of features titled the "Language Acquisition Device" nor to disrespect the massive body of work on linguistic anthropology, cognitive linguistics, and the philosophy of language.

There are other ways in which the argument I have presented may lend itself to misinterpretation, especially in light of previous objections to Whorfianism and the defenses its adherents are accustomed to bringing up. For example, the traditional insistence that no one has claimed that language absolutely determines thought is not useful here. That kind of claim is a straw-man argument that almost no one has made, so evidently false that engaging it would serve little purpose. In my introduction, I acknowledge that no Whorfians make such simplistic claims, and instead present a more specific argument: that even the notion of language making people significantly more "likely" to think in certain ways is highly fraught— for example, in the claims it forces us into on Chinese and East Asian languages.

Finally, I have not dismissed academic work showing that the workings of a language can have some effect on thought. Repeatedly I have acknowledged and praised these studies, such that I have tried to enforce a distinction between academic and popular Whorfianism. Therefore: in response to a possible observation that I have not done Whorfian experiments myself, with the implication that if I did so I would find evidence of language's influence on thought, I agree wholeheartedly! The evidence from the studies is so obvious, in itself, that it would be quite unnecessary for me to go out and repeat their results with other languages. The work has been done.

My interest is in the implications we are taught to draw from the elegant but whispery results in question. Yes, whispery—the psychologist will work with them, but the problem is this "worldview" business promoted to those of us out there in the dark. One may delight in the variety among the world's languages without basing that delight in an idea that each language's individual workings create a different lens on life. My argument has been that it is preferable to sidestep that tempting frame of mind. Science does not support it in the way that it is promulgated beyond the ivory tower. It entails a view of other people that should be suspicious to all both within and beyond that ivory tower. Plus it just isn't necessary. My work, like that of countless others, has been an attempt to show interested people that languages are fascinating in their own right.

We are told that what languages teach us about being human is how different we are. Actually, languages' lesson for us is more truly progressive—that our differences are variations on being the same. Many would consider that something to celebrate.

Notes

Introduction

The truth about Hopi: Ekkehart Malotki, *Hopi Time: A Linguistic Analysis of the Temporal Concepts in the Hopi Language* (Berlin: Mouton de Gruyter, 1983), 534.

Hoijer on Navajo: Harry Hoijer, "Implications of Some Navaho Linguistic Categories," in *Language in Culture and Society*, edited by Dell Hymes, 142–28 (New York: Harper & Row, 1964).

Deutscher, "Color may be the area...": Guy Deutscher, *Through the Language Glass: Why the World Looks Different in Other Languages* (New York: Metropolitan Books, 2011), 231.

Everett on cultural cloaks: Dan Everett, *Language: The Cultural Tool* (New York: Pantheon, 2012), 324.

Whorf on Newtonian science: John B. Carroll, ed., *Language, Thought, and Reality: Selected Writings of Benjamin Lee Whorf* (Cambridge, MA: MIT Press, 1956), 154.

Pinker on Whorfianism: Steven Pinker, *The Stuff of Thought: Language as a Window into Human Nature* (New York: Viking, 2007), 124–50.

Jakobson, "languages differ essentially...": Roman O. Jakobson, "On Linguistic Aspects of Translation," in *On Translation*, edited by R. A. Brower, 232–39 (Cambridge: Harvard University Press, 1959), 236.

von Treitschke, "differences of language...": Heinrich von Treitschke, *The History of Germany in the Nineteenth Century*, edited by Gordon Craig (Chicago: University of Chicago Press, 1975), 327.

Chapter 1

Casasanto study: Daniel Casasanto, "Space for Thinking," in *Language, Cognition, and Space: State of the Art and New Directions*, edited by V. Evans and P. Chilton, 453–78 (London: Equinox Publishing, 2010).

Pinker while writing *The Stuff of Thought*: Steven Pinker, *The Stuff of Thought: Language as a Window into Human Nature* (London: Allen Lane, 2007), 124.

The Herero people: Guy Deutscher, *Through the Language Glass: Why the World Looks Different in Other Languages* (New York: Metropolitan Books, 2011), p. 62, citing Hugo Magnus, *Untersuchungen über den Farbensinn der Naturvölker* (Jena: Gustav Fischer, 1880), 9.

Pirahã: What kicked off the media storm was Peter Gordon, "Numerical Cognition without Words," *Science* 306 (2004): 496–99. The more general portrait of Pirahã and its peculiarity compared to Western ones was Dan Everett, "Cultural Constraints on Grammar and Cognition in Pirahã: Another Look at the Design Features of Human Language," *Current Anthropology* 46 (2005): 621–46.

Pirahã and numbers: The handiest source for getting a look at the controversy is Andrew Nevins, David Pesetsky, and Cilene Rodrigues, "Pirahã Exceptionality: A Reassessment," *Language* 85 (2009): 355–404, esp. 384–85, and Everett's reply, equally key to evaluating the issue, Daniel Everett, "Pirahã Culture and Grammar: A Response to Some Criticisms," *Language* 85 (2009): 405–42, esp. 424–25.

Pinker on snow: Pinker, *The Stuff of Thought*, 125–26.

Guugu Yimithirr: Stephen C. Levinson, "Relativity in Spatial Conception and Description," in *Rethinking Linguistic Relativity*, edited by John J. Gumperz and Stephen C. Levinson, 177–202 (Cambridge: Cambridge University Press, 1996), 180–81.

Tzeltal: Penelope Brown and Steven Levinson, "'Uphill' and 'Downhill' in Tzeltal," *Journal of Linguistic Anthropology* 3 (1993): 46–74.

The table experiment: with the Tzeltal, Peggy Li and Leila Gleitman, "Turning the Tables: Language and Spatial Reasoning," *Cognition* 83 (2002): 265–94; with the Tzotzil, Leila Gleitman, Peggy Li, A. Papafragou, C. R. Gallistel, and L. Abarbanell, "Spatial Reasoning and Cognition: Cross-linguistic Studies," University of Pennsylvania Department of Psychology presentation slides, 2005.

Japanese experiment: Mutsumi Imai and Dedre Gentner, "A Crosslinguistic Study of Early Word Meaning: Universal Ontology and Linguistic Influence," *Cognition* 62 (1997): 169–200.

How other people with number/stuff languages feel: John A. Lucy, *Language Diversity and Thought: A Reformulation of the Linguistic Relativity Hypothesis* (Cambridge: Cambridge University Press, 1992), 146.

Yucatec: Lucy, *Language Diversity and Thought*, 140–41.

Mandarin debate: Lera Boroditsky, "Does Language Shape Thought? Mandarin and English Speakers' Conception of Time," *Cognitive Psychology*

43 (2001): 1–22, and David January and Edward Kako, "Re-evaluating Evidence for Linguistic Relativity: Reply to Boroditsky (2001)," *Cognition* 104 (2006): 417–26.

Boroditsky's reply: Lera Boroditsky, Orly Fuhrman, and Kelly McCormick, "Do English and Mandarin Speakers Think about Time Differently?" *Cognition* (2010) (online publication).

Chapter 2

Whorf on patterns: John B. Carroll, ed., *Language, Thought, and Reality: Selected Writings of Benjamin Lee Whorf* (Cambridge, MA: MIT Press, 1956), 252.

Comment on Rossel Island language: Beatrice Grimshaw, *Guinea Gold* (London: Mills & Boon, 1912), 191–92.

Tuyuca evidential markers: Janet Barnes, "Evidentials in the Tuyuca Verb," *International Journal of American Linguistics* 50 (1984): 255–71.

Korean kids and evidential markers: Anna Papafragou, Peggy Li, Youngon Choi, and Chung-Hye Han, "Evidentiality in Language and Cognition," *Cognition* 103 (2007): 253–99.

The distribution of evidential markers: Martin Haspelmath, Matthew S. Dryer, David Gil, and Bernard Comrie, *The World Atlas of Language Structures* (Oxford: Oxford University Press, 2005), 316–17.

Articles worldwide: Frans Plank and Edith Moravcsik, "The Maltese Article: Language-Particulars and Universals." *Rivista di Linguistica* 8 (1996): 183–212.

Eating verbs in New Guinea and Jarawara: Alexandra Aikhenvald, "'Eating,' 'Drinking,' and 'Smoking': A Generic Verb and Its Semantics in Manambu," in *The Linguistics of Eating and Drinking*, edited by John Newman, 91–108 (Amsterdam: John Benjamins, 1996).

Nunamiut and Tareumiut: Allen Johnson and Timothy Earle, *The Evolution of Human Societies: From Foraging Group to Agrarian State* (Palo Alto: Stanford University Press, 1987).

Dropping *t*'s and *d*'s: Gregory Guy, "Variation in the Group and the Individual: The Case of Final Stop Deletion," in *Locating Language in Time and Space*, edited by William Labov, 1–36 (New York: Academic Press, 1980).

Berber: E. Destaing, *Vocabulaire Français-Berbère: Étude sur la tachelhît du soûs* (Paris: Librairie Ernest Leroux, 1938).

Harrison: K. David Harrison, *The Last Speakers: The Quest to Save the World's Most Endangered Languages* (Washington, DC: National Geographic, 2010), 237–38.

Chapter 3

You in Chinese: Susan D. Blum, "Naming Practices and the Power of Words in China," *Language in Society* 26 (1997): 357–79.

Ethnography of communication: The classic anthology, including an article on the Kuna of Panama, is Richard Bauman and Joel Sherzer, *Explorations in the Ethnography of Speaking* (Cambridge: Cambridge University Press, 1974).

The Kuna: The detailed treatment, as opposed to the article-length one in the source above, is Joel Sherzer, *Kuna Ways of Speaking* (Austin: University of Texas Press, 1983).

Adults streamlining languages: I discuss this in my books *Our Magnificent Bastard Tongue: A New History of English* (New York: Gotham Books, 2008) and *What Language Is (And What It Isn't and What It Could Be)* (New York: Gotham Books, 2011). I also recommend Peter Trudgill, *Sociolinguistic Typology: Social Determinants of Linguistic Complexity* (Oxford: Oxford University Press, 2011).

Chapter 4

Atsugewi sentence: Leonard Talmy, "Semantic Structures in English and Atsugewi," PhD dissertation, University of California, Berkeley, 1972.

Whorf on less complex languages: John B. Carroll, ed., *Language, Thought, and Reality: Selected Writings of Benjamin Lee Whorf* (Cambridge, MA: MIT Press, 1956), 83.

Bloom study: Alfred H. Bloom, *The Linguistic Shaping of Thought: A Study in the Impact of Language on Thinking in China and the West* (Hillsdale, NJ: Lawrence Erlbaum, 1981).

Responses to Bloom: Terry Kit-Fong Au, "Chinese and English Counterfactuals: The Sapir-Whorf Hypothesis Revisited," *Cognition* 15 (1983): 155–87; Terry Kit-Fong Au, "Counterfactuals: In Reply to Alfred Bloom," *Cognition* 17 (1984): 289–302; L. G. Liu, "Reasoning Counterfactually in Chinese: Are There Any Obstacles?" *Cognition* 21 (1985): 239–70; Donna Lardiere, "On the Linguistic Shaping of Thought: Another Response to Alfred Bloom," *Language in Society* 21 (1992): 231–51; David Yeh and Dedre Gentner, "Reasoning Counterfactually in Chinese: Picking Up the Pieces," *Proceedings of the Twenty-Seventh Annual Meeting of the Cognitive Science Society*, edited by B. G. Bara, L. Barsalou, and M. Bucciarelli, 2410–15 (Mahwah, NJ: Lawrence Erlbaum and Associates, 2005).

Oral culture and questions: Shirley Brice Heath, *Ways with Words: Language, Life, and Work in Communities and Classrooms* (Cambridge: Cambridge University Press, 1983).

Peasants and puzzles: Alexandr Romanovich Luria, *Cognitive Development: Its Cultural and Social Foundations*, edited by Michael Cole, translated by Martin Lopez-Morillas and Lynn Soltaroff (Cambridge, MA: Harvard University Press, 1976).

Gendered things: Lera Boroditsky, Lauren A. Schmidt, and Webb Phillips, "Sex, Syntax, and Semantics," in *Language in Mind: Advances in the Study of Language and Thought*, edited by Dedre Gentner and Susan Goldin-Meadow, 61–79 (Cambridge, MA: MIT Press, 2003).

Dinka plurals: D. Robert Ladd, Bert Remijsen, and Cahuor Adong Manyang, "On the Distinction between Regular and Irregular Inflectional Morphology," *Language* 85 (2009): 659–70.

Laotian sentence: N. J. Enfield, *A Grammar of Lao* (Berlin: Mouton de Gruyter, 2007), 530.

Future tense and savings rates: Keith Chen, "The Effect of Language on Economic Behavior: Evidence from Savings Rates, Health Behaviors, and Retirement Assets," Cowles Foundation Discussion Paper no. 1820, Yale University, August 2012.

Number words in Chinese and Thai: Fabian Bross and Phillip Pfaller, "The Decreasing Whorf-effect: A Study in the Classifier Systems of Mandarin and Thai," *Journal of Unsolved Questions* 2 (2012): 19–24.

Chapter 5

Black English and logic: Carl Bereiter, Siegfried Englemann, J. Osborn, and P. A. Reidford, "An Academically Oriented Pre-school for Culturally Deprived Children," in *Pre-school Education Today*, edited by Fred M. Hechinger, 105–36 (Garden City, NJ: Doubleday, 1966).

Jensen position: Arthur Jensen, "How Much Can We Boost IQ and Scholastic Achievement?" *Harvard Educational Review* 39 (1969): 1–123.

Jarawara *they:* R. M. W. Dixon, *The Jarawara Language of Southern Amazonia* (Oxford: Oxford University Press, 2004), 77–88.

Abley on Algonquian: Mark Abley, *Spoken Here: Travels Among Threatened Languages* (Boston: Houghton Mifflin, 2003), 276–77.

Manambu in the night: Alexandra Y. Aikhenvald, *The Manambu Language East Sepik, Papua New Guinea* (Oxford: Oxford University Press, 2008), 522.

Whorf on Hopi and flying things: John B. Carroll, ed., *Language, Thought, and Reality: Selected Writings of Benjamin Lee Whorf* (Cambridge, MA: MIT Press, 1956), 210.

Verbs of knowing: Abley, *Spoken Here*, 48.

Chapter 6

Abley on Mohawk: Mark Abley, *Spoken Here: Travels Among Threatened Languages* (Boston: Houghton Mifflin, 2003), 188–89.

Wilson on Russian: Lewis A. Dabney, *Edmund Wilson: A Life in Literature* (New York: Farrar, Straus & Giroux, 2005), 409.

Kawesqar: Jack Hitt, "Say No More," *New York Times*, February 29, 2004.

Generic pronouns as sexist: Megan M. Miller and Lorie E. James, "Is the Generic Pronoun He Still Comprehended as Excluding Women?" *American Journal of Psychology* 122 (2009): 483–96.

Koasati: Mary Haas, "Men and Women's Speech in Koasati," in *Language in Culture and Society*, edited by Dell Hymes, 228–33 (New York: Harper & Row, 1964).

Kūrux: Francis Ekka, "Men and Women's Speech in Kurux," *Linguistics* 81 (1972): 21–31.

Treatment of women in feminine-default languages: Dan Everett, *Language: The Cultural Tool* (New York: Pantheon, 2012), 209–10.

On Australian languages and time: Wade Davis, *The World Until Yesterday*, by Jared Diamond (book review), *The Guardian*, January 9, 2013.

Get in English: Anna Wierzbicka, *English: Meaning and Culture* (Oxford: Oxford University Press, 2006), 171–203.

Get languages: N. J. Enfield, "On Genetic and Areal Linguistics in Mainland South-east Asia: Parallel Polyfunctionality of 'Acquire,'" in *Areal Diffusion and Genetic Inheritance*, edited by Alexandra Y. Aikhenvald and R. M. W. Dixon, 255–90 (Oxford: Oxford University Press, 2001).

Haitian pronouns: Amy Wilentz, *Farewell, Fred Voodoo* (New York: Simon & Schuster, 2013), 82.

Lakoff: The book-length presentation was George Lakoff, *Don't Think of an Elephant: Know Your Values and Frame the Debate* (White River Junction, VT: Chelsea Green Publishing, 2004).

Brown's universals: Donald E. Brown, *Human Universals* (Philadelphia: Temple University Press, 1991), 130–41.

Lahu sentence: James A. Matisoff, "Lahu," in *The Sino-Tibetan Languages*, edited by Graham Thurgood and Randy J. LaPolla, 208–21 (London: Routledge, 2003), 219.

Saramaka artists: Sally Price and Richard Price, *Maroon Arts: Cultural Vitality in the African Diaspora* (Boston: Beacon Press, 1999), 132–33.

Testicles and months in Lahu: James A. Matisoff, *The Grammar of Lahu* (Berkeley: University of California Press, 1973), 147–48.

Index